D0313003

PRAISE FOR *4 CHAIR DISCIPLING*

Of all the disciplers I know, my friend Dann Spader is at the top of the list. He disciples with his life, through his seminars and workshops, and now, thankfully, through this powerful book. Highly recommended!

Joe Stowell I President, Cornerstone University I Grand Rapids, Michigan

Few people have the reputation of Dann Spader—with a life's passion for making disciples. Now in *4 Chair Discipling,* Dann challenges us to walk more faithfully in Jesus' calling. Read and dwell on this helpful book.

Ed Stetzer I President I Lifeway Research

Dann Spader's giftedness and knowledge have been a huge help to Southeast Christian Church. His *4 Chair Discipling* can be an enormous benefit to your church as well. Learn to make disciples who make disciples by studying how Jesus modeled it for all of us. It's a journey you'll want to take!

Dave Stone I Senior Pastor of Southeast Christian Church I Louisville, Kentucky

Dann Spader and Sonlife played a part in our journey here at Real Life to discover a reproducible discipleship model that would work in a church. Dann has been committed to doing discipleship Jesus' way, and he has inspired many to follow suit. For those who have listened it has been life and ministry changing. He is one of the voices that should be heard in a church culture badly in need of Jesus and His methods for discipleship. I encourage you to read what he has to write.

Jim Putman I Senior Pastor I Real Life Ministries I Post Falls, Idaho

Who could deny that the responsibility to make disciples would be at the top of the list of what Jesus wants/commands His people to do?

Yet, who would deny that most of us don't know quite what that is or how to do it? Dann Spader's *4 Chair Discipling* blends rich biblical instruction and insight along with skilled and fruitful experience to help Christians understand and embrace the call to make disciples.

Following Jesus requires this of us, and Spader's work provides hope and confidence in understanding how Jesus would have us to proceed.

Bruce A. Ware I Professor of Christian Theology I Southern Seminary I Louisville, Kentucky I
Author of *The Man Christ Jesus: Theological Reflections on the Humanity of Christ*

Dann Spader has taken the popular concept of "servant leadership" and created a very practical and sustainable method for discipling people to actually BECOME servant leaders. Spader's *4 Chair Discipling* is a highly effective way to model and implement Jesus' approach and command for making disciples. This work is much needed, long overdue, and could serve as a core approach for discipling and apprenticing in any growing ministry or church.

Jon Ferguson I Community Christian Church I Naperville, Illinois I New Thing Network

My friend Dann Spader, is passionate about making disciples. And his latest book, *4 Chair Discipling*, captures a simple and powerful way to become more effective in making this happen. I highly commend it to you.

Josh McDowell I Author of more than eighty books including
More Than a Carpenter and *New Evidence that Demands a Verdict*

Dann Spader has spent a lifetime studying, coaching, and carrying out Jesus's call to make disciples. In *4 Chair Discipling*, he explores the disciple-making methods Jesus used and shows how they are still the prototype for today. With powerful *aha* analogies and illustrations, he presents a biblical and practical pathway and template for making disciples. If you want to become a better disciple maker, this book is a must-read.

Larry Osborne I Author and pastor I North Coast Church I Vista , CA

For over 30 years, Dann Spader has been a bold and clear voice calling the church to a disciple-making movement and not just programmatically producing disciples. The *4 Chair Discipling* book is refreshing, informative, and practical in helping us see disciple-making in the simple genius of Jesus and His way of life in making disciples who make disciples. This is a must-read for pastors, church leaders, and families.

Fritz Dale I Executive Director of Reach National I Evangelical Free Church

Dann Spader is passionate about walking as Jesus walked! In *4 Chair Discipling* you will be encouraged and inspired to do what Jesus did. This is one of the most practical books I've read on how to multiply disciples. It will instruct and inspire you to walk like Christ!

Ken Adams I Senior Pastor of Crossroads Church and President of Impact Ministries I Newnan, Georgia

Through a careful study of the life of Christ over the past 40 years, Dann Spader has captured Jesus' strategy of making disciples. *4 Chair Discipling* is not theory, it is what Dann has been living for over 30 years of ministry. Drawing a distinction between disciple-making and discipleship, this book is a must-read for any pastor, youth pastor, small group leader or Christian leader serious about fulfilling the Great Commission.

Dr. Bob MacRae I Professor of Youth Ministry I Moody Bible Institute

I happen to believe the church in North America has grown increasingly inward, often untethering our spiritual life from our mission. As I read my friend Dann's book, I found myself praying: "God, give me and us this vision, passion, and clarity for making disciples who make disciples." Dann is spot on and prescribes exactly what we need. Thanks, Dann, for putting your finger on first things and arguing biblically and specifically about what making disciples looks like in practice.

Rob Bugh I Senior Pastor Wheaton Bible Church I Wheaton, Illinois

As a pastor of a lifegroup church in Atlanta, I look forward to all my leaders going through Dann Spader's new book *4 Chair Discipling*. It's a winner! Just what I've been waiting for—practical, fast-moving, biblical, interactive, missional, and life-giving.

Fred Hartley I Lead Pastor and author of *God on Fire* I Tucker, Georgia

Dann's passion for growing a disciple-making movement comes through loud and clear in his book *4 Chair Discipling*. His passion for people to know the real Jesus compels the reader to want to be a part of a disciple-making community. If you take the Great Commission seriously, then read the book.

Dr. Mark A. Hoeffner I Executive Director, CB Northwest I Teaching Pastor, Grace Baptist Church I White Salmon, Washington

Nothing has shaped my ministry philosophy more than Dann Spader's profound teaching on the life of Jesus. If you desire to bear lasting fruit, read this book as soon as possible!

With deep insight and practical examples, Dann shows us how to make disciples like Jesus did. More than just a theorist, he personally lives out these principles in daily life, with amazing results. A must-read, *4 Chair Discipling* could well be the most important ministry book you encounter this year.

Dave Patty I President of Josiah Venture I Eastern Europe

Making disciples can get confusing and complicated. So many books, theories, and programs can leave people wondering where to start. But Dann has articulated in a simple way how every person and every church can begin to make disciples like Jesus made disciples. With just four chairs, you will be equipped to move people along their way to walking as Jesus walked.

We use the four-chair strategy in our church, and it has given us a new language to talk about disciple-making and a simple tool to cast vision. I highly recommend this resource to any leader who wants to ignite movements by making disciples.

Craig Etheridge I Senior Pastor I First Baptist Church I Colleysville, Texas

Dr. Dann Spader has been a global force for the cause of Christian disciple-making. *4 Chair Discipling* provides a simple, easily transferable, and proven method for discipling that can be used by pastors, youth workers, and volunteers in a wide range of cultural contexts. This book will help Christian leaders succeed in the primary purpose of their work: to make disciples of Christ.

Terry Linhart, PhD I Author, educator I Bethel College, Indiana

This book deeply impacted my life and in turn the ministry I lead.

We all live in houses but few know how to actually construct one. As Christian leaders we exist in the church but few know how to make disciples.

Out of years of experience, Dann teaches us how to make disciples following the pattern of Jesus. He shows us how to practically "swing a hammer."

Dean Plumlee I National Director I Christian Surfers USA

What the church needs now is a fresh understanding of an old truth. How do we grow up as believers and become the disciple-makers that Jesus intended for us to be? And how do we help others do the same? Dann has spent a lifetime casting vision on this subject and on the life of Christ. Filled with great stories and personal insight, *4 Chair Discipling* is an essential read for everyone who wants to be a fully devoted follower of Jesus. It digs deep and yet provides a simple and clear demonstration of how we can walk others through the phases of spiritual development.

Dale Edwardson I National Church Health Director I C&MA

I have interacted with Dann Spader. I have listened to his heart and mind, and I know him as an undisputed leader in disciple-making. He is a disciple who lives what he preaches. His teaching on the humanity of Christ and its implications has totally changed my reading of the gospels.

Dann's book is an exceptionally practical guide to disciple-making. The *4 Chairs* speak to every culture and language. It is especially welcome in my continent, Africa, a continent with huge numbers of daily conversions but very few models of effective disciple-making. It is a tool for pastors and marketplace leaders across the globe that I highly recommend.

Since I first heard it from Dann, I have used this model with the men we minister to in different churches in Kenya with awesome results. Thanks Dann and thanks to God, for a book so simple yet so profound. May God use it to prepare the bride for the Groom!

The book is easy to read, a needed challenge to the casual reader of the gospels, and a model and guide for the Christ-follower. Awesome work indeed!

Simon Mbevi I Pastor and Executive Director of Transform Kenya Initiative

For thirty years I have watched Dann go deeper into his study of the life and methods of Jesus. Now, in this book, he takes the fruit of that lifelong journey and translates it into a highly reproducible strategy for making disciples. His "four chairs" paradigm frees us from the box of programmatic thinking and gives us an easily accessible process that could fit any church or ministry environment. The renewed global attention on disciple-making might be the most important conversation of the decade. *4 Chair Discipling* couldn't come at a better time.

Dr. Gary Mayes I VP Church Resource Ministries I Author, *DNA of a Revolution: 1st Century Breatkthroughs That Will Transform the Church*

Disciple-making is the primary mission of the church. Before Jesus ascended to heaven, He commanded His followers to make disciples of all nations. Yet some well-meaning churches neglect, if not miss out on this Great Commission.

In his book *4 Chair Discipling*, Dann unearths timeless discipleship treasures from the ultimate model of disciple-making—Jesus, the Master Discipler. Knowing Dann personally, he is a practitioner of what he is writing. I highly recommend this book not just to pastors and church leaders, but also to all laymen and laywomen who want to take the call to make disciples of prime importance in their lives and in their churches!

Dr. Peter F. Tan-chi I Senior Pastor I Christ's Commission Fellowship I Manila, Philippines

It is unlikely that we can make disciples unless we can describe what a disciple looks like and the process of how a disciple is made. Dann's life and ministry have been devoted to exemplifying this process.

In this book he has given a simple description of the process that is rooted in the life of Christ using the four chairs. This book will help you return to the disciple-making process that Jesus modeled. It is a must-read!

Andrew Tay I President, Intentional Disciple Making Network I Singapore

Dann Spader is not just a recognized leader rich with insights from the study of Jesus life and leadership; he is a practitioner, disciple-maker, and movement builder.

This practical book will extend his contribution to the fruitfulness of other leaders globally as they seek to coach people through the Four Chair process of becoming disciple-makers bearing much fruit.

Bill Hodgson I Campus Crusade for Christ Australia

In a world saturated with leadership models, there is a scarcity of attention and examination given to the life and methods of Jesus. Spader leads us to a clear understanding of Christ's methods. I am indebted to Spader for the ways in which his life and leadership have shaped me and countless others.

Steve French I President I Lifework Leadership I Orlando

4 Chair Discipling

Growing a Movement of Disciple-Makers

Dann Spader

MOODY PUBLISHERS
CHICAGO

All Scripture quotations, unless otherwise indicated, are taken from the *Holy Bible, New International Version*®, NIV®. Copyright © 1973, 1978, 1984, 2011 by Biblica, Inc.™ Used by permission of Zondervan. All rights reserved worldwide. www.zondervan.com. The "NIV" and "New International Version" are trademarks registered in the United States Patent and Trademark Office by Biblica, Inc.™

Scripture quotations marked NASB are taken from the *New American Standard Bible*®, Copyright © 1960, 1962, 1963, 1968, 1971, 1972, 1973, 1975, 1977, 1995 by The Lockman Foundation. Used by permission. (www.Lockman.org)

Scripture quotations marked ESV are taken from *The Holy Bible, English Standard Version*. Copyright © 2000, 2001 by Crossway Bibles, a division of Good News Publishers. Used by permission. All rights reserved.

Scripture quotations marked KJV are taken from the King James Version.

Scripture quotations marked CEV are taken from the *Contemporary English Version*. Copyright © 1991, 1992, 1995 by American Bible Society. Used by permission.

Scripture quotations marked EXB are taken from *The Expanded Bible*. Copyright © 2009 by Thomas Nelson, Inc. Used by permission. All rights reserved.

Edited by Brandon J. O'Brien
Cover design: Faceout Studio/Tim Green
Chairs photos: Getty Images, image #171987832
Interior design: Design Corps

Library of Congress Cataloging-in-Publication Data

Spader, Dann.
  Four chair discipling : growing a movement of disciple-makers / Dann Spader.
    pages cm
  Includes bibliographical references and index.
  ISBN 978-0-8024-1207-2 (alk. paper)
  1. Discipling (Christianity) I. Title.
  BV4520.S624 2014
  253—dc23
                                     2014001582

We hope you enjoy this book from Moody Publishers. Our goal is to provide high-quality, thought-provoking books and products that connect truth to your real needs and challenges. For more information on other books and products written and produced from a biblical perspective, go to www.moodypublishers.com or write to:

Moody Publishers
820 N. LaSalle Boulevard
Chicago, IL 60610

3 5 7 9 10 8 6 4

Printed in the United States of America

Dedicated to the 1000s of young leaders
around the globe involved with Global Youth Initiative.
Your passion and fruitfulness in making disciples has truly shaped
my life and inspired our family.

Especially to my dear friend Mark Edwards,
who first introduced me to using four chairs to explain the Life of Christ.
From the days of being your youth pastor to watching you lead your own
movement of disciple-makers, you have been used by God to
impact my life. I'm indebted to you.

To my supporters who have made it possible for me to lock myself in a
room and write. You know who you are, and God knows. May your eter-
nal rewards surpass your greatest dreams. You give so sacrificially.
Without you, I could not be leading GYI.

And finally, to our new friends at Southeast Christian Church.
You have modeled a passion to know Jesus that is contagious. Char and
I have felt truly loved and welcomed. It has been a joy working with your
gifted staff and leaders in teaching the Life of Christ
and disciple-making.

I'm excited about what the Lord has in store.

For videos and more resources
visit: 4chairdiscipling.com

CONTENTS

CHAPTER ONE

Where It All Began

grew up in a large family. When I say, "large," I mean *very* large.
My parents had sixteen children. I was number fifteen of sixteen,
so I'm glad that my parents had so many children, or I would not be
here! All of my brothers and sisters, except for the oldest three, have
first names that begin with the letter "D." We always joked that we
wanted the last child to be called "Done."

When child number sixteen was born, my mom went off to the
hospital (only the last few were born in the hospital) and we heard
through the grapevine that it was a boy. Everyone was excited! This is
"Done"!

By the time my mom and dad arrived home, the whole family was
eagerly waiting to see if our new brother was named Done. Dad delivered the news sheepishly: "We named him Dallas."

Everyone was disappointed. "Why didn't you call him Done?" they
asked.

Dad looked up with a twinkle in his eye and said, "Well, to be honest, we aren't sure we are done yet!"

Even though I was the next-to-last child born, as far as I know, I
was the first in my family to come to a clear understanding of what it
means to become a Christ-follower. It happened while I was attending
an engineering school in South Dakota. In order to catch a free ride to
his hometown to see his girlfriend, my roommate, also named Dann,
decided it was worth it to tolerate seven hours in a car with a bunch of
"Jesus freaks." During the weekend, Dann and his girlfriend couldn't

find anything fun to do, so they attended the very first Campus Crusade for Christ conference (CRU) in the state. Dann accepted Christ that night, and it changed his life! Immediately when he returned to our fraternity house, I noticed a change in his life. One night after a keg party, I came back to our room and found him reading a Bible.

"What happened to you?" I asked. "Why are you reading that?"

With trembling hands, he pulled out a Four Spiritual Laws tract and began to read it to me. He was so nervous that I had to hold the booklet so he could read it.

The Holy Spirit moved that night. On December 17, 1970, at 9:43 p.m., I bowed my head with my roommate, repented of my sin, and asked Christ to take control of my life.

My roommate and I began reading the Bible together, and we were thrilled by what we found. One evening we got so excited when we discovered that the story of Noah and the ark was a true story in the Bible! And because of the Spirit's work in our lives, we saw that story in a totally new way. We wept for joy because we had been rescued from the judgment of sin.

We went up and down the halls in our fraternity house and read the Four Spiritual Laws booklet to anyone who would listen. Several prayed to receive Christ and—because we had been Christians and studying the Scriptures just a few weeks longer than they had—we led the Bible studies.

It didn't take me long to realize that I needed some training, both in ministry and understanding the Scriptures. I hardly knew the difference between the Old Testament and the New Testament, much less how to interpret them. So I left engineering school and headed to Bible school. Much to my surprise, a small church on the north side of Chicago offered to pay me money to minister to their youth! *I should be paying you*, I thought. *But if you want to pay me to practice on your kids, I'll take it.*

One day in a class on the gospel of John, my professor, Stan Gundry, made a statement in passing that changed my life. "Some of Christ's first disciples could have been teenagers," he said.

This totally changed my perception of Jesus! I thought Jesus was an old guy (I was only twenty at the time) and that His disciples were old guys. But when I realized that John could have been in his late teens, and several of the other disciples could have been in their late teens or early twenties, I was amazed! I was working with students the same age. Maybe I could learn to lead my youth group by exploring how Jesus worked with His youth group!

After class I rushed up to my professor and asked how I could learn more. He encouraged me to study the life of Christ chronologically. Dr. Gundry had just compiled a harmony of the Gospels, which looks at Christ's life chronologically, and he encouraged me to get a copy.[1] Study what Jesus did the first year, he advised. Where did He go? What did He say? Why did He do the things He did? Then do the same with the second year and the third year. He encouraged me, in short, to study the Son's life.

This set me on a journey that became my life passion. We named our youth group Sonlife—we were just trying to live out the Son's life. For twenty-five years I led a ministry called Sonlife, through which we trained countless numbers of youth pastors and pastors in the Son's life. Over the years I've discovered that Jesus modeled a very simple pattern for disciple-making, a pattern every Christian can easily imitate. Jesus's disciple-making strategy follows four challenges He posed to His followers: "come and see" (John 1:39), "follow me" (John 1:43), "follow me and I will make you fishers of men" (Matthew 4:19), and "go and bear fruit" (John 15:16). With this simple pattern, Jesus led His disciples through the natural growth process from children, to young men, and to spiritual fathers. This book is dedicated to explaining this simple process. In chapter 4 we will introduce four chairs as a simple metaphor to explain this disciple-making process. These four chairs will reflect the four challenges of Jesus, a simple transferable metaphor of how Jesus developed "fully trained disciples" (Luke 6:40).

THE MESSAGE OF JESUS

Unfortunately, it took me many years to discern this very simple pattern. For the first ten years I studied the life of Christ, I focused mainly upon His message—the words of Jesus. Twenty percent of the words in the New Testament are the words of Jesus. One in every four verses in the New Testament is quoting the sayings of Jesus. That's a lot of material!

Jesus's message is profound. He spoke in simple terms. He spoke, for example, of the "lilies of the field," the "birds of the air," and "the sowers and the seed." But His simple words carried profound weight. People were "amazed" at Jesus's words, for "he spoke with authority," unlike the other teachers of the Law (Mark 1:22). But I would argue that if you completely understand the message of Christ but fail to understand His methods, you won't truly know the Jesus of the Scriptures. Jesus was much more than just His words and message.

THE METHODS OF JESUS

For the next ten years of my Christian life, I focused on the methods of Jesus. I studied to identify His major priorities and analyze them in His life and ministry. I wrote a Harmony self-study, which explained what I consider the strategy of Jesus.[2] We trained tens of thousands of youth pastors, pastors, and church leaders in the methods of Christ. Some of those methods included:

Jesus was deeply committed to relational ministry. John 3:22 tells us that Jesus "spent time with his disciples." The Greek word translated "spent time with" here is *diatribo*. It means "getting under the skin of." Jesus gave His disciples time to get to know Him and took time to invest in them.

Jesus invested early in a few. Within eighteen months of beginning His ministry, Jesus identified five individuals (James and John, Simon and Andrew, and Matthew) and challenged them to go deeper with Him. Even before He chose His twelve disciples, Jesus deepened His investment in these few, teaching them how to be "fishers of men."

Jesus often slipped away to pray. More than forty-five times in the Gospels, Jesus escaped the crowds to pray. The busier He became the more He prayed. His ministry began with prayer and ended with prayer. Before every major turning point in Jesus's life, He spent focused time in prayer.

Jesus loved sinners profoundly. Jesus was described as a "friend of sinners." His opponents used that title to condemn Him, but Jesus wore it as a badge of honor. He associated with those others condemned. He befriended those others despised. He was always drawn to the neediest, not to the sharpest.

Jesus balanced His efforts to win the lost, build believers, and equip a few workers. Jesus understood that His mandate was to "make disciples." Disciple-making for Jesus meant meeting the needs of people where they were spiritually and then challenging them to the next level. His goal was multiplication, and with laser focus He trained His few disciples to multiply their lives in others. And in the Great Commission, which is a great summary of His life, He told His disciples to go and repeat the process with others.

JESUS'S MODEL FOR DISCIPLE-MAKING

Jesus, as the perfecter of our faith, develops us to become "fully trained disciples," reflecting His character and priorities completely (Luke 6:40). In order to perfect the faith of His disciples, over a period of more than three years, Jesus modeled a pattern for us to study and follow. Unfortunately, it has been my experience in training leaders in disciple-making that very few look to Jesus as the model of how to do this! There are several reasons for this.

Many people fail to recognize Jesus's intentional disciple-making process because they don't expect to find a pattern in Jesus's ministry. Few have analyzed what He did with His disciples the first year, the second year, and then the third year. More than 80 percent of the books I've read about Jesus in the last forty years talk about the message of Jesus. The rest of them may also allude to some of the methods of Jesus. But I can only identify four major books that look deeply at Christ's life as the pattern for disciple-making.[3]

Others are resistant to the very idea that the Gospels contain a pattern for disciple-making. They argue the Gospels were never intended to be studied that way. "If God wanted us to study Jesus's life chronologically," I've heard many people object, "He would have given us a chronological record of the life of Jesus." There is a simple response to this objection: He has! Luke begins his gospel with this explanation: "Therefore, since I myself have carefully investigated everything from the beginning, it seemed good also to me to write an orderly account for you, most excellent Theophilus" (Luke 1:3). Luke researched the life of Christ by consulting eyewitnesses and weighing their testimony (1:2) and studying historical documents comprehensively. Once he compiled his information, he made an orderly account of Jesus's life. The Greek word *kathexes*, translated "orderly account," indicates a successive, or chronological, record.

Chronology is important because it gives us insight we could not gain in any other way. For example, without a chronological understanding of Jesus's life, few realize that Mark 1:17, where Jesus tells His disciples "follow me and I will make you fishers of men," is not His first connection with these disciples. At that point, they had been with Jesus for at least eighteen months, and now He is calling them to a new level of involvement and development. When Jesus chose the twelve apostles (Luke 6:12–16), He had been investing in them for two and a half years. Understanding the chronology of Jesus's life helps us to understand how He developed His disciples. This book explores this chronology to identify disciple-making Jesus style.

But perhaps the greatest roadblock that keeps people from studying the life of Christ as their model for disciple-making is an underlying assumption that few people will openly state. It goes like this: *I really can't do what Jesus did. He was God. I can't do what God does!* One young man said to me after a recent training event, "Dr. Spader, you state over and over again that we should 'do what Jesus did.' While I like what you are saying, my problem is simply this: He was God and I'm not!"

I appreciated this young man's honesty. His concern is one I've heard before. However, his objection is rooted in a faulty view of the real Jesus. It has been my experience in North America (not so much in other parts of the world) that many Christians imagine Jesus to be some sort of Superman. He may *appear* to be a human—a Clark Kent by day—but this humanity is a disguise. In actual fact, Jesus is a caped wonder, a superhero with superpowers. This is poor theology! Jesus was no super man. He was *fully* human. And that distinction is critical.

If we believe that Jesus was superhuman, we may likewise conclude that it is therefore impossible to do what He did.

Paul did not view Jesus in this way. He understood Jesus as a very real person, set in time and space. He understood both His humanity and deity and told us that this Jesus, the real Jesus of the Bible, is the Jesus that we are commanded to imitate. We are commanded to "walk as He walked" (1 John 2:6). We are to follow the very pattern of His life that He so powerfully modeled to the first-century disciples, the pattern they so clearly recorded in the Gospels, under the influence of the Holy Spirit. "That which we have heard, that which we have seen with our eyes, which we have looked at and our hands have touched," John wrote, "this we proclaim" (1 John 1:1). I love how Philippians 2:5 says it: "think the same way that Christ Jesus thought" (CEV) or "think and act like Christ Jesus" (EXB).

In the next chapter, I want to begin to explore a critical aspect of the "real Jesus." It's important that we discuss this aspect before we move on to talk about Jesus's model for disciple-making, because a wrong view of Jesus will lead to a misunderstanding of disciple-making. I'm convinced that you can't get to know that real Jesus until you understand both His deity and His humanity. His deity is profound. Jesus *is* God Himself. But the reality that Jesus "became flesh and made his dwelling among us," adding humanity to His deity, adds a whole new dimension to the real Jesus (John 1:14). We cannot possibly "think and act" just like Jesus if we only understand the message of Jesus. We cannot even "think and act" just like Jesus if we understand both the message and methods of Jesus. In order to "walk *as* He walked" (1 John 2:6) and "do what Jesus did" (John 14:12) we must understand the real Jesus who walked on this planet over 2,000 years ago. To "think and act" like the real Jesus, we must clearly understand His full humanity. In the next chapter we will begin to explore that profound mystery.

PONDERINGS

1. How do you react to the author's personal journey of moving from the message to the methods to the very model of Jesus's life? Have

you found anything similar in your own Christian journey? How has your understanding of Jesus developed as you've matured as a Christian?

_____

_____

_____

2. Look up Philippians 2:5 in several different translations (the simplest way to do this is on a website such as BibleGateway.com). In the space below, write out two or three translations of this verse that impact you especially. What do you find interesting or challenging about this verse of Scripture?

_____

_____

_____

3. What could happen in a person's life if she fully lived out this verse? What does the context of Philippians 2 tell us about how to do this?

_____

_____

_____

_____

CHAPTER TWO

The Full Humanity
of Jesus

What if it were possible to do what Jesus did? What if, like Jesus, we could make a major impact on our world without ever traveling more than a hundred miles from home? What if we could take a group of "unschooled and ordinary men" and equip them to turn the world upside down (Acts 4:13)? What if in just four short years we could create a movement of disciple-makers, just like Jesus? If I told you all this is possible, would you do it?

These may sound like extraordinary claims. But Scripture makes some extraordinary claims, too. In John 14:12, for example, Jesus explains that "whoever believes" in Him will do the works He did during His earthly ministry. But Jesus doesn't stop there. In the second half of John 14:12, He goes on to say that His disciples will do "even greater things" than He did!

You may find this hard to believe. Jesus did some incredible works, beyond just His miracles. He took ordinary men and transformed them into world changers. So even if you believe that the Bible is true—even if you take Jesus at His word—you may imagine you could never do the things Jesus did, not to mention doing *greater* things. For many years of my Christian walk, I knew I was supposed to imitate Jesus, but deep inside I believed that Jesus did what He did because He was God. Obviously, I am not! So I worked hard with very little confidence that I would ever succeed. What I know now is that my mistaken view of Jesus was crippling my disciple-making.

FULLY GOD AND FULLY MAN

Ever since I became a Christian, I have held a deep conviction that Jesus was fully God, a conviction that originates in the Bible's teaching about Jesus. Jesus clearly claimed to be equal with His Father. In John 10:30 He says that to see Jesus is to see the Father. Moreover, Jesus claimed to exist prior to His incarnation. Jesus proclaims in John 8:58, "I tell you the truth, before Abraham was born, I am." The Jews to whom Jesus was speaking recognized the phrase "I Am" as referring to the name of God from the Old Testament (Exodus 3:14) and to the theistic proclamations in the latter part of Isaiah (Isaiah 41:4 and 60:16). The Jewish officials understood Jesus's meaning completely; that's why they wanted to execute Him for blasphemy! "For this reason," John explains, "the Jews tried all the harder to kill him; not only was he breaking the Sabbath, but he was even calling God his own Father, making himself equal with God" (John 5:17–18). Of course, the Jewish officials did not believe Jesus's claim to divinity. They considered Him a "mere man" who simply *claimed* to be God (John 10:33).

Jesus clearly claimed to be God, received worship as God, and was crucified because of His claims to be God. Furthermore, Jesus's earliest followers acknowledged that Jesus was fully God. Paul makes this clear in Philippians, where he commends his readers, "Your attitude should be the same as that of Christ Jesus: who, *being in very nature* God, did not consider equality with God something to be grasped" (Philippians 2:5–6, italics added). He put the matter even more clearly in Colossians 2:9: "For in Christ all the fullness of the Deity lives in bodily form."

Can we all agree the Bible teaches that Jesus was fully God?

Jesus's true identity is complicated by the fact that while the Bible clearly teaches that Jesus was fully God, at the same time the Scripture is also clear that Jesus was fully human. Hebrews 2:17 claims that "he was like us in all ways." Throughout Jesus's life and ministry, He experienced emotions and sensations that every one of us has experienced in our lives. He was conceived by and born to an ordinary woman (Matthew 1:18; Luke 1:31; Matthew 1:16, 25; 2:2; Luke 2:7, 11). He "grew in wisdom and stature," which means He grew physically and intellectually (Luke 2:52). He became hungry and thirsty (Matthew 4:2; 21:18;

John 4:7; 19:28). He became weary and He slept (John 4:6; Matthew 8:24; Mark 4:38). He felt sorrow and grief, and when a dear friend of His died, He wept (Isaiah 53:3–4; Luke 22:44; John 11:33; 12:27; Luke 19:41; John 11:35).

Even in those situations which we will likely never experience, Jesus demonstrated His full humanity. During His arrest, trial, and execution, Jesus endured all manner of indignities (Luke 23:11). Soldiers spat in His face and punched Him (Matthew 26:67; Luke 22:64). He was flogged with a whip (Matthew 27:26; John 19:1), nailed to a cross (Luke 23:33), and run through with a spear (John 19:34). Jesus's human body responded to these assaults the way ours would. He was bloodied and bruised and He ultimately died (John 19:30) and was buried (Matthew 27:59–60; Mark 15:46). The New Testament is clear: Jesus fully partook of our flesh and blood (John 1:14; Hebrews 2:14). He was a real human being. In all ways except for our sinfulness, Jesus was just like us (Hebrews 4:15).

THE CHALLENGE OF TWO NATURES

You may be beginning to sense a problem at this point. How can Jesus be "fully God" and "fully man" at the same time? How could Jesus possibly maintain His divine nature at the same time that He lived in a human body?

Consider this example:

Does God know all things? Of course! The Bible teaches clearly that God is omniscient, that there is nothing He does not know. But was Jesus, the human Jesus, omniscient? Scripture indicates that He was not. He did not know the time of His return (Matthew 24:36). He did not know "who touched me" until someone told Him (Luke 8:45). He did not know that His cousin John had been beheaded until someone reported the news to Him (Matthew 14:8, 12). The fact that Jesus grew "in wisdom and stature, in favor with God and man" demonstrates that in His humanity He did not know all things automatically but had to learn, just like you and I. As a matter of fact, Jesus clearly said, "everything that I learned from my Father I have made known to you" (John 15:15). Just as you and I learn, Jesus learned about His Father and His Father's will through Scripture, prayer, and the Holy Spirit.

In other words, as God Himself, Jesus should know all things. But as a human being, His knowledge was limited, just as ours is. Are you beginning to scratch your head?

Here's another example: God is omnipotent—He is all-powerful and He can do all things. But was Jesus able, in His humanity, to do everything He needed or wanted to do? Mark records one episode in which Jesus visited His hometown and, "He could not do any miracles there, except lay his hands on a few sick people and heal them" (Mark 6:5).

Let me offer one more example. Scripture tells us God is omnipresent—He is everywhere and sees all things. But Jesus, in His humanity, was not. In fact, Jesus experienced grief—and caused His good friends grief—precisely because He was not omnipresent. While Jesus was teaching in one town, Jesus's close friend Lazarus passed away in another town. When He arrived to Bethany, where Lazarus lived, Lazarus's sister told Jesus, "if you had been here, my brother would not have died" (John 11:21).

Do you see the problem? How can Jesus be "fully God" and "fully man" at the same time? How can He know all things in His divinity and yet not know all things in His humanity? How can He be present everywhere and yet not present everywhere? How can He be all powerful and yet have real human limitations?

THE KENOSIS OF JESUS

In Philippians 2:5–11, the apostle Paul gives us a glimpse into the solution to the problem of how Jesus can operate both as fully God and fully human. Paul uses the Greek word *morphe*, which means "nature" or "substance," twice in this passage. He uses it first in verse 6, where it refers to the nature (*morphe*) of God. The second time he uses it is in verse 7, where it refers to the nature (*morphe*) of man. Both verses are describing Jesus. This Jesus, Paul writes, "being in very nature (*morphe*) God, did not consider equality with God something to be grasped, but made himself nothing, taking the very nature (*morphe*) of a servant, being made in human likeness."

In other words, Jesus is fully equal to God in every way. Jesus shares the same essential divine nature (*morphe*) as God the Father. But incredibly, Jesus also shares with us a human nature (*morphe*) because He chose to become like us. Paul tells us in verse 7 that Jesus, even though He is fully God, "emptied himself" or "made himself nothing" taking the very nature of a servant!

How did the Son add humanity to His deity? Theologians, at the Council of Chalcedon in 451 A.D., struggled to articulate how this could work. Up to that point there were those who denied the deity of Jesus (Ebionites and Arianism) and there were also those who denied the humanity of Jesus (Docetism and Appolinarianism). Each of these faulty views had been defined as heresy. The members of the council drafted a statement that finally refuted these heretical views, summarizing the views of Christians before them and setting the standard for Christological orthodoxy for many years to come. The Chalcedon statement reads:

> We, then, following the holy Fathers, all with one consent, teach men to confess one and the same Son, our Lord Jesus Christ, the same perfect in Godhood and also perfect in manhood; truly God and truly man, of a reasonable (rational) soul and body; con substantial (co-essential) with the Father according to the Godhood, and con substantial with us according to the Manhood: in all things like unto us, without sin; begotten before all ages of the Father according to the Godhood, and in these latter days for us and for our salvation, born of the Virgin Mary, the Mother of God according to the Manhood; one and the same Christ, Son, Lord, Only-begotten, to be acknowledged in two natures, inconfusedly, unchangeable, indivisibly, inseparably; the distinction of natures being by no means taken away by the union, but rather the property of each nature being preserved, and concurring in one Person (prosopon) and one Subsistence (hypostasis), not parted or divided into two persons, but one and the same Son, and only begotten, God the Word, the Lord Jesus Christ, as the prophets from the beginning (have declared) concerning him, and the Lord Jesus Christ himself has taught us, and the Creed of the holy Fathers has handed down to us."[1]

In an attempt to explain how Jesus could be fully God and fully man at the same time, the theologians at Chalcedon came up with a statement that has stood the test of time. They stated that Jesus decided in eternity past that when He added humanity to His deity, He would veil His deity so that His humanity could find full expression. The theologians who met at Chalcedon knew that we cannot affirm the humanity of Jesus in a way that sacrifices the deity of Jesus.

Jesus, the Son, became human—*fully* human—but He did so in a way that preserved His deity. To accomplish this, something drastic had to happen. Philippians 2:7 tells us what that was: "God made himself nothing, taking the very nature of a servant." God chose to temporarily cloak His deity, to veil it, in order that His humanity could find full expression. By adding humanity, He chose temporarily to restrict the full expression of His deity. Never less than God, He chose to live His life never more than man. As Bruce Ware has said, "His Deity was unexpressed, so that His humanity could find full expression."[2]

Imagine with me for a moment a king who rules a vast kingdom. This king had everything a king should have: servants who waited on him, a rich wardrobe, and vast banquets for every meal. Everything that he ever desired was brought to him. One day, as he was surveying his kingdom, he observed beggars in the street. He felt pity and wanted to help them. But how? The only way to really help these homeless people, he realized, was to become like them. So while still remaining king, retaining every right, authority, and all the riches of his kingdom, he took off his royal garments and put on the clothes of a beggar. Then he left the comforts of his castle and became a vagabond.

The king lived exactly as the beggars lived, surviving on the generosity of strangers and sleeping in the cold streets. People passed by him, mocked and spat on him. The king suffered greatly. As king, he could have called for his army at any time to retaliate against the people who treated him unjustly. But he chose not to, for if he did he could not fully experience life as a beggar. The homeless can't call for the royal army to protect them. The king never stopped being king, and he never relinquished his authority over his kingdom. Nevertheless, to fully experience the beggar's life, he refused to exercise the rights that were his as king.

This is a picture of what the incarnation is all about. Christ, who is eternal God, became flesh and dwelt among us. Though He was rich, for our sakes He became poor. He did this so that through Him, we who were poor might become rich.

WHAT DOES ALL THIS MEAN?

Haddon Robinson has said that most errors in Bible teaching are not made in the exegesis of a text but in the application of the text to life. With this caution in mind, we have to ask, What does this work of Jesus mean for us? How does it affect our Christian journey to know that Jesus was fully human while He remained fully divine?

1) Jesus did not dip into His deity to live out His humanity. Like the king who set aside his royalty to live among the poor, Jesus never took advantage of his divinity to live out His humanity. If He had, He would not have been fully human. He would not have been like us in every way (albeit without sin). He would have been less or more (depending upon your perspective) than human. But Scripture is clear that Jesus "shared in our humanity" and that He was "made like his brothers in every way" (Hebrews 2:14, 17).

Imagine a credit card. Imagine Jesus carrying the ultimate Master-Card, the God card. The number on it is 777-7777-777. The expiration date is eternity. The credit limit is infinity, for He owns it all and made it all. Jesus had the God card when He lived on this earth, because He was fully God. But in order to be like us in every way, He chose never to use it. And thank God that He didn't! If Jesus had not lived a truly human life, He could not have redeemed us from our sins. "If Christ did not become fully human," wrote Gregory of Nazianzus, "then His redemption of man could not have been fully complete."[3] Satan seems to have understood this, because when he tempted Jesus in the wilderness, he tried to convince Jesus to use the God card. "If you are the Son of God," Satan taunted, "tell these stones to become bread" (Matthew 4:3). Jesus replied the way all of us should—by acknowledging that our strength and hope come only from the Word of God.

What a profound thought! Jesus, who was God Himself, experienced all of life just as we do. He did not utilize His divine power to live out His human life on earth. Yet He lived a life free of sin. From the first minute of His life, all the way to His final breath on the cross, Jesus lived in reverent submission to His Father and obeyed Him in all aspects! He did it all without dipping into His deity to live out His humanity! The first human being, Adam, had the chance to live a life without sin. But he failed when he broke fellowship with God. Jesus was the second Adam, and He accomplished what Adam failed to do, remaining obedient even to death on the cross (Romans 5:12–20).

You may be thinking, *Surely Christ's miracles are proof that Jesus used His God card.* Jesus could not have done all of His miracles without using His divine powers, right? Not necessarily. Christ's miracles were not proof of His deity. Instead, they are proof of His Messiahship (Luke 5:24; Matthew 11:4–5). The Israelites expected the Messiah to perform miracles to help people recognize who He was. Think about it: the apostles in the book of Acts duplicated most of the miracles Jesus performed. They healed the sick and raised the dead, just as Jesus had. They even performed miracles Jesus never attempted, such as speaking in tongues (Acts 2:7–8). Doing all this did not prove that they were divine. Moses performed miracles. So did Elijah. Working wonders does not prove that a person is divine. It proves that they are yielded to what God has chosen to do through them for His purposes.

Jesus's miracles were proof that He is the Christ sent from His Father (John 10:25). Jesus tells us in His own words that He did nothing by His own power. Everything He did was done by the Father and in submission to His Father's desires. "I tell you the truth," Jesus said, "the Son can do nothing by himself; he can do only what he sees his Father doing" (John 5:19). Jesus was clear that "By myself I can do nothing" (John 5:30). Even Jesus's teaching was not His own. It "comes from him who sent me" (John 7:16). Jesus wanted His disciples, and even His opponents, to recognize that His miracles were testimony not to His own power or authority but to the power and authority of God the Father: "The words I say to you are not just my own. Rather, it is the Father, living in me, who is doing his work. Believe me when I say that I am in the Father and the Father is in me; or at least believe on the evidence of the miracles themselves" (John 14:10–11). At the end of His ministry Jesus was confident that His disciples, at least, recognized that the source of His miraculous deeds was God Himself (John 17:7).

Jesus, as the second Adam, in reverent submission to His Father, became a conduit of the power of His Father, as everything He did was done in acknowledgment of His Father's work. In the same way, Jesus instructed His disciples that they should relate to Him the way He related to His Father. Just as Jesus modeled total dependence on the Father, He told us, "apart from Me you can do nothing" (John 15:5). Jesus's disciples, in the book of Acts, followed Christ's example by acknowledging every miracle as coming from God working through them. After healing a crippled beggar, Peter clarified that he was not the one who worked the miracle. "Men of Israel," he said, "why does this surprise you? Why do you stare at us as if by our own power or godliness we had made this man walk?" (Acts 3:12).

If Jesus's miracles do not prove that He occasionally used His God card, then what about the special knowledge He demonstrated? Jesus predicted events before they happened. He read people's thoughts and peered into their hearts. Don't these acts prove He used His deity to live out His humanity?

Not necessarily.

Eleven different times in the Gospels it is recorded that Jesus knew something that others did not seem to know. On five occasions He knew people's thoughts (Matthew 12:24–25; Luke 5:22; 6:7–8; 11:16–17). In Mark 2:6-8, for example, "some teachers of the law were sitting there, thinking to themselves, 'Why does this fellow talk like that? He's blaspheming! Who can forgive sins but God alone?' Immediately Jesus knew in his spirit that this was what they were thinking in their hearts."

It may seem that Jesus used His divinity to read His opponents' thoughts. But there are other ways He could have known what they were thinking. His Father could have revealed their thoughts to Him by the Holy Spirit. Proverbs tells us that the Lord takes the upright into

His confidence (Proverbs 3:32). Amos 3:7 reports that the "Sovereign Lord does nothing without revealing his plan to his servants." Surely the Spirit of God could have given Jesus a discerning spirit to know men's hearts.

There is, of course, another option. Perhaps Jesus sensed something in the teachers' countenance or the posture of their body. Jesus was sinless and had perfect discernment. Couldn't this discernment give Him a quick understanding of their thoughts and intentions? On three occasions it says that Jesus "knew all men" (John 2:23–24) or "knew their hypocrisy" (Mark 12:15). Any mature believer who understands the Scriptural teaching about human nature could make the same observation. Surely we can conclude that Jesus "knew what was in men" because He understood the Scriptures profoundly.

The Bible tells us that Jesus "grew in wisdom and stature, and in favor with God and men" (Luke 2:52). In other words, just like you and I, Jesus developed intellectually, physically, spiritually, and socially. Like any human, Jesus studied the Scriptures, grew in wisdom, and allowed the Spirit to guide him into all truth. He was not downloaded as a little baby with biblical data. He learned as He lived among us (John 15:15). The Scriptures and the Holy Spirit were all available to Jesus in His humanity, just as they are available to all Christians today. This leads us to another astounding conclusion about the humanity of Jesus.

2) The resources that Jesus had available to Him are the resources available to you and me. Even though Jesus never used the God card, He nevertheless had access to some incredible resources. In fact, throughout His ministry, Jesus had access to four resources to which all Christians also have access.

The first was the Holy Spirit. Every aspect of Jesus's life was saturated with the Holy Spirit. We are told that He was conceived by the Spirit (Luke 1:35), anointed by the Spirit (Luke 4:18; Acts 10:38; Isaiah 11:1–2) and even "filled with the Spirit" (Luke 4:1, 14; John 3:34). Jesus was also sealed by the Spirit (John 6:27) and led by the Spirit (Luke 4:1). In Luke 10:21 we are told He "rejoiced in the Spirit" and even "performed miracles by the power of the Spirit" (Matthew 12:28). Paul records in Romans that Jesus was "raised by the Spirit" (Romans

8:11). If the living Son of God, in all His greatness, chose not to live without the constant help of the Spirit for even one moment, how can we do any less?

Second, Jesus relied on prayer. More than forty times Scripture tells us that Jesus "often withdrew to lonely places and prayed" (Luke 5:16). Jesus's ministry began after forty days of fasting and prayer (Luke 4:1–11), and Jesus ended His ministry in prayer (Luke 23:46–47). It was while Jesus was praying that the Spirit came upon Him (Luke 3:21–22). It was after a season of prayer that Jesus walked on the water (Matthew 14:25), chose His twelve apostles (Luke 6:12), showed compassion on a woman caught in adultery (John 8:1–10), and faced the horror of the cross (Matthew 26:36–46). For Jesus, prayer was a source of strength to resist temptation (Matthew 26:41) and an opportunity to learn His Father's desires (Mark 1:38) and listen to His Father's words (John 12:49–50).

Third, Jesus had access to the written Word of God. On over ninety occasions it is recorded that Jesus quoted the Old Testament Scriptures, referring to seventy different Old Testament chapters. He knew the Scriptures, studied them, and used them in the everyday events of life. The Word had center stage in Jesus's life and ministry. Three times in John 13 it is said that Jesus "knew" that the time had come, that the Father had put all things under His power, and who was going to betray Him. Why? Because He studied the Scriptures. Jesus knew the events before Him because He clearly studied and knew the Scriptures must be fulfilled (Matthew 26:54, 56; Mark 14:27; Luke 22:36–37; John 19:24, 28).

Jesus demonstrated the depth of His understanding of the Scriptures after His resurrection when, on the road to Emmaus, Jesus explained the entire Bible to a couple of His disciples. "Beginning with Moses and all the Prophets, he explained to them what was said in all the Scriptures concerning himself" (Luke 24:27). With His disciples later on, Jesus reiterated this truth: "This is what I told you while I was still with you: Everything must be fulfilled that is written about me in the Law of Moses, the Prophets and the Psalms" (Luke 24:44).

Finally, Jesus had access to supportive friends and family. Even though Christ's brothers were not initially supportive of His ministry, Jesus gained strength from His family and parents. Mary and Joseph were obviously a source of strength when Jesus was younger. Even up until His crucifixion on the cross Jesus was concerned for Mary's care. Jesus's twelve disciples were a source of both great joy and great sorrow. But in Jesus's own words they moved from just followers (John 1:43), to servants (John 13:13, 16), to friends (John 15:15), and then brothers (John 20:17). Hebrews 2:11 tells us that Jesus was not ashamed to call us His brothers.

Every aspect of Jesus's ministry was relational. To Jesus, relationships were not a strategy; they were part of being fully human. Just as God the Father is in community in the Trinity, so God the Son established a community of brothers. Jesus drew strength from those relationships (Matthew 26:36–38) and told us not to "give up meeting together" but to "encourage one another" (Hebrews 10:25). The early church in Acts clearly understood this resource (Acts 2:42).

3) Jesus is my model for life and ministry. Bruce Ware, Professor of New Testament at Southern Seminary, explains the significance of Jesus's earthly obedience in this way:

> So many people minimize or demean the obedience of Christ by saying, 'Of course He obeyed. He was God and had God's nature in Him. He had no choice.' Scripture does not let us draw this conclusion. It presents Christ as a man who faced every temptation and succeeded not because He relied on His divine nature, but because He relied upon the Word, prayer and the Spirit. And He succeeded all the way to the cross, even to death on the cross."[4]

The beauty of Christ's life is that He modeled how to live life in total dependence upon the Father. Jesus showed us how to live as humans: fully dependent, fully obedient, fully reliant upon the Word of God, Spirit of God, and prayer. Ian Thomas, founder of Torchbearers International, used to say, "Jesus was man as God intended man to be." Sure, Jesus was sinless and we are sinful. But as we mature, we should sin less. When in doubt, don't ask WWJD (what *would* Jesus do). First study to see WDJD (what *did* Jesus do). Jesus showed us how to live in a sin-soaked world, and He did it perfectly. Our ultimate goal is to become like Him in every thought and deed.

4) We underestimate what God wants to do through us. Jesus is my model for life and ministry. He is alive and wants to lead us today! He leads us through the very model of His life written in His Word, the power of His resurrected life interceding for us, and the very presence of His Holy Spirit indwelling us. Because of this resurrected power and His indwelling presence, we tend to underestimate what God wants to do through us.

On seven different occasions Jesus rebuked His disciples for their lack of faith (Matthew 6:30; 8:26; 13:58; 14:31; 16:8; 17:20; Mark 16:14). Twice He challenged them saying, *"Are you still so dull?"* (Matthew 15:16).

In Matthew 17, a man brings to Jesus his demon-possessed son. The man says that he had asked the disciples to drive out the spirit, but they could not. Jesus, with grief in His heart, said:

> "You unbelieving and perverse generation, how long shall I stay with you? How long shall I put up with you? Bring the boy here to me." Then the disciples came to Jesus in private and asked, "Why couldn't we drive it out?" He replied, "Because you have so little faith. Truly, I tell you, if you have faith as small as a mustard seed, you can say to this mountain, 'Move from here to there,' and it will move. Nothing will be impossible for you."

I personally believe that the greatest grief we bring to the heart of Jesus is our lack of faith in what He wants to do in and then through us. We underestimate what God wants to do!

In the upper room on the night before He was crucified, Jesus's last words to His disciples were peppered with a simple command: "ask." Six different times Jesus tells His disciples to simply "ask" (John 14:13, 14,16; 15:16; 16:23, 24)! We so often underestimate what God wants to do through us. And because of this, we look at the mission of Jesus as beyond our ability. This is a mistake. Grasping the greatness of the command to simply "ask," we can now approach the mission Jesus has given us with great joy and anticipation, because we know now, like Jesus in His humanity, that the power is not within us, but within the resources that He has made available to us!

Empowered with these resources, we are ready to embark on His mission, motivated by His love, to make disciples according to His model.

PONDERINGS

1. What questions do you still have about Christ's humanity/deity? How would you articulate the relationship between Jesus's divine and human natures?

_____

_____

_____

2. How does this chapter change or challenge your understanding about Jesus and the mission He has given us?

_____

_____

_____

3. Read Hebrews 2:8–18 and Hebrews 5:7–10. How do these verses reinforce what this chapter is saying?

_____

_____

Visit www.4ChairDiscipling.com for more resources.

CHAPTER THREE

Our Mission and Motive

Once we grasp the significance of the full humanity of Jesus, we are now poised to begin to understand Jesus's commands in the Great Commission and the Great Commandment. In fact, we can't truly understand or fulfill these commands until we fully understand Jesus's humanity.

As we shall discover in detail in just a moment, the Great Commandment is to love God and love people (Matthew 22:36–40). The Great Commission is to make disciples (Matthew 28:18–20). These two statements alone encompass the greatest of all commitments modeled by our Savior. During His earthly ministry, Jesus loved God, loved people, and made disciples. And He calls us to do the same. To put it another way, the Great Commandment speaks to the motive of our disciple-making. We are motivated by love of God and love for people. The Great Commission speaks to our mission. We are sent to make disciples. Fortunately Jesus modeled for us how exactly how to do this!

THE GREAT COMMISSION

Every four years the summer Olympics begins with an event that captures the imagination of the world: the lighting of the Olympic flame. At the end of an international marathon relay, one final runner enters the Olympic stadium. After traveling by foot, by bicycle, by boat, or by air, sometimes over thousands of miles, the torch finally enters the stadium in the hands of a final runner who, to the thrill of millions, ignites the enormous Olympic flame.

Wouldn't it be exciting to be one of the bearers of the flame? Picture it. Each stride throbs with a sense of mission. Your fingers carefully encircle this forged symbol of Olympic competition. All fatigue fades as adrenaline fills you for this once-in-a-lifetime moment. Your experience would be a family legend. Grandkids would show your picture to their friends and boast, "That's my grandpa (or grandma) there. He carried the torch to the Olympics!" Can you imagine holding that piece of tradition in your hands and knowing that, for a brief moment, you were the link in that historic chain?

As Christians, we carry a torch.

We carry a flame of so much greater value that there is no comparison. The pomp and circumstance of the Olympics pales against the eternal significance of the ministry with which Christ has entrusted us. Proud athletes carry the Olympic torch accompanied by global applause, while Christians through the ages have borne the torch of the gospel despite centuries of persecution and trial. The flame we carry is not a symbol. It is the light of God that is desperately needed by a dark and dying world.

There is no better way to rediscover passion for the life we've been given to live than to return to the point where Jesus first passed the torch to His disciples. Understanding what He said in that pivotal moment will enable us to clearly understand our mission in this life.

THE ORIGINAL HANDOFF

Matthew records the words we call the Great Commission at the very end of his gospel. They were probably among Jesus's very last words to His disciples. Last words tend to be very important words. I clearly remember my father's last words to me over twenty years ago. He carefully chose words he knew I needed to hear. Words he wanted me to remember and live by. Words he lived his life by. I believe Jesus did the same.

The fact that we call this passage the Great Commission may intimidate you. The word "great" may make you think that this commission is given to "great" Christians or "great" missionaries. That's not me! I can't do that!

But Jesus's last words to His disciples were nothing more than a few short words designed to summarize Christ's life. The disciples' job, Jesus was saying, was to do for the rest of their lives what He had done in His. It was an everyday commission, given to every believer for every moment of his or her life. Jesus is charging His disciples to make other disciples who will make even more disciples, just as Jesus did. The Great Commission is every Christian's task.

Let's take a closer look at these final verses of Matthew. It was a day of challenge, a day for handoff. From the very beginning Jesus had told His disciples of His desire to make them "fishers of men." He had involved them in ministry. He had taught them His priorities and allowed them to observe Him in action. But things were different now. He had been crucified and raised from the dead, and the time for His ascension was near.

Over the course of forty days between His resurrection and His ascension, Jesus appeared to His disciples approximately ten times. Sometimes He appeared to individual disciples, sometimes to a group of them. Only once does Jesus announce His appearance before it happens, and this is the time, this meeting in Galilee. Excitement was running high. The women disciples were spreading the news that the angel had given them: "Go and tell my brothers to go to Galilee; there they will see me" (Matthew 28:10).

Who all was Jesus planning to meet that day? I am convinced this was the gathering of the 500 that is referenced in 1 Corinthians 15:6. Matthew writes, "Then the eleven disciples went to Galilee, to the mountain where Jesus had told them to go" (Matthew 28:16). This doesn't mean that only eleven disciples total were present with Jesus that day. It simply could mean that the eleven had to travel from Jerusalem to Galilee, but there were already disciples in Galilee. I believe there were at least another 489 present. This is significant because many argue that Jesus's (Great) Commission was only given to the Eleven, Jesus's closest companions. In reality, Jesus gave this charge to every Christ-follower. The commission is "great" because it has to do with the gospel. Even so, it is an everyday commission for every believer for every moment of their everyday lives.

It is important to recognize, too, that Jesus did not commission His disciples to take on this task in their own strength. Before He commands His listeners to make disciples, He tells them, "All authority in heaven and on earth has been given to me" (Matthew 28:18). After the commission, he assures them, "I am with you always, to the very end of the age" (28:20). Wrapped around this Great Commission is a promise of the active and manifest presence of the Lord. This is no small promise! Jesus invites us to share His life, His passion, His calling. And He promises that any person, any family, any church that commits itself to doing what Jesus did can expect and claim that active manifest Presence in their midst! Jesus loves to show up in a supernatural way when we seek to do what He did.

TWO COMMANDS AND THREE VERBS

The Great Commission contains two commands and three action words. The first command is simply to "make disciples." This single activity was the driving focus of Jesus's life. Jesus poured His life into a few disciples and taught them to make other disciples. Seventeen times we find Jesus with the masses, but forty-six times we see Him with His disciples. These few disciples, within two years after the Spirit was poured out at Pentecost, went out and "filled Jerusalem" with Jesus's teaching (Acts 5:28). Within four and a half years they had planted multiplying churches and equipped multiplying disciples (Acts 9:31). Within eighteen years it was said of them that "they turned the world upside down" (Acts 17:6 ESV). And in twenty-eight years it was said that "the gospel is bearing fruit and growing throughout the whole world" (Colossians 1:6). For four years Jesus lived out the values He championed in His Everyday Commission. He made disciples who could make disciples!

The commission continues with three verb forms that modify the first command. These three verbs—go, baptize, and teach to obey—give us the three priorities of disciple-making.[1] Although the Great Commission is usually translated, "Go and make disciples," the verb for "go" is better translated "going" or "as you go." In other words, the "going" Jesus is talking about is not a special event, such as a mission trip. Instead, we are to make disciples as we go to work, as we go to school, as we go out into our neighborhood. As you go, walk as Jesus walked! This truly is an everyday command you are to live every day *as you go*—wherever you go.

"Baptizing" is a critical element of disciple-making. It indicates identifying publicly with the work and cause of Christ. When a person comes to faith in Christ, they must then be baptized to identify externally with a change that has taken place internally. Baptism is an important external expression of an internal identity as a Christian.

Teaching others to obey "everything I have commanded you" involves a lifetime of following and learning from Christ. Jesus gives more than 400 commands in the gospels and more than half of them are disciple-making commands. Becoming a disciple of Jesus does not mean completing a curriculum or attending a church activity. It is a lifestyle of becoming more like Jesus. As we learn to live a lifestyle of obedience we bear fruit, *more* fruit, and then *much* fruit (John 15:1–8). God multiplies our lives and our effectiveness to the ends of the earth, so that we can make disciples of all nations.

We can do what Jesus did if we walk as Jesus walked. In fact, we can even do greater things than Jesus did. Jesus had only four years to make disciples. By God's grace we can have forty years or more to make disciples. But we *must* do what He did and walk as He walked. The rest of this book is dedicated to explaining how Jesus did what He did. The place to begin is to recognize that we share the same mission that Jesus had: making disciples who can make disciples.

But before we move on, let's give attention to one more little detail in Matthew 28:18–20. For years I taught that there was only one command in this everyday commission. But upon further study and the help of a studious businessman, I realized that there is a second command in this text that most people miss.

One reason we miss this second command is because of how it is often translated in English. It is the little Greek word *idou*, which is translated in many Bibles as "surely" or "lo," as in, "Surely I am with you always." In the Greek language, *idou* is a command (in the imperative mood in Greek). The New Living Translation captures this second and powerful command: "And be sure of this: I am with you always, even to the end of the age" (Matthew 28:20). In essence Jesus is saying, As you make disciples you *must* keep focused on Me. As you commit to this type of lifestyle, don't you forget that I will be with you and I will show you how to do this! I will make you disciple-makers!

THE GREAT COMMANDMENT

While the Great Commission deals with our mission, the Great Commandment speaks to our motives. The Great Commission establishes our priorities. The Great Commandment clarifies our passion.

Jesus summarized all the Law and the Prophets, all the teaching of the Old Testament with profound simplicity: "Love the Lord your God with all your heart and with all your soul and with all your mind. This is the first and greatest commandment. And the second is like it: Love your neighbor as yourself" (Matthew 22:37–40). Love is the greatest Christian motive. To commit to making disciples without love makes all our efforts sound to God like a resounding gong or a clanging symbol (1 Corinthians 13:1). Without love we are nothing and can gain nothing (1 Corinthians 13:2–3).

Walking as Jesus walked means walking in love. This love includes a deep love for God emblazoned upon our whole heart, soul, mind, and strength. This love also includes loving people. Loving people involves both tenderness and toughness, both graciousness and truthfulness at the same time. Moreover, loving God means loving people, and loving people means loving God. You cannot separate the two. God is love and love comes from God. Loving God results in loving people. First John 4:20–21 (ESV) tells us plainly, "If anyone says, 'I love God', and hates his brother, he is a liar; for he who does not love his brother whom he has seen cannot love God whom he has not seen. . . . Whoever loves God must also love his brother."

It is natural to wonder which people we are supposed to love. In Luke 10, an expert in religious law questioned Jesus about how to live out this Great Commandment. He wanted to know who Jesus meant, exactly, when He commanded us to "love your neighbor." "Who is my neighbor?" the lawyer asked.

Jesus answered by sharing the parable of the Good Samaritan, which teaches that anyone who crosses your path and has needs is your neighbor. Then Jesus changed the question. The key question according to Jesus is not "Who is my neighbor?" but "Who is a good neighbor?" In the parable, it was the Samaritan who reached out and helped. It was the Samaritan who saw the need and moved toward the needy person. It was the Samaritan who gave what he had to help the person in need. He approached and embraced the person in need, whereas the other characters in the story retreated. Love was the difference—a love that manifested itself in compassion and mercy.

The Great Commission and the Great Commandment must be held together in one thought. Because we love God, we love people. Because we love people, we make disciples. To try to make disciples without love gains nothing. And if we say we love people but never try to make disciples, then our love is a lie. As we love God, we will love people. As we love people the way God loves us, we will be engaged in making disciples. The two go together and make the journey simple, not complicated.

Our motive drives our mission. Our passion fuels our priorities. Our heart energizes our hands. Loving God and loving people is our motive. Making disciples who can make disciples is our mission. Throughout His ministry, Jesus modeled what it means to love God and love people, and through His priorities He made disciples who made disciples. Then, in His final words to His disciples—including you and me—He summarized His mission and handed it off to us to complete.

In the next few chapters, we will look at the specific methods by which Jesus made disciples. It is a simple process I call 4 chair discipling.

PONDERINGS

1. Read Matthew 28 and Luke 10:25–42. What does it look like to focus on "making disciples" (Matthew 28:16–20) without a Great Commandment heart? Be specific.

_____

_____

_____

_____

_____

_____

2. What is the difficulty of trying to live out the Great Commandment, if you have no clear understanding of how Jesus made disciples?

_____

_____

_____

_____

3. Read Luke 10:38–42. How does this story illustrate the importance of living out the Great Commission with a Great Commandment heart? What can we learn from the real-life situation of Mary and Martha as we try to live like Jesus did?

_____

_____

_____

_____

CHAPTER FOUR

The Method—an Overview

Plants follow a natural growth process that is referenced frequently in Scripture. A seed, unless it dies and germinates (John 12:24), can be taken away by the birds of the air and never reproduce (Mark 4:4). But once that seed falls to the ground, dies, and germinates, it can establish roots, grow, and bear fruit, more fruit, and even much fruit (John 15:1–8). The germinated seed reproduces and multiplies itself thirty, sixty, or even a hundredfold (Mark 4:20).

Jesus understood that just as plants follow a natural, organic process of development, so too can human disciples. John alludes to this organic discipling process in 1 John 2:12–14, where he talks about the natural growth process of disciples from children to young men (women) and, finally, to fathers (parents). Jesus did not take any shortcuts with this process. Instead, He developed His disciples naturally and intentionally. Moreover, He instructed us to follow His pattern of disciple-making. One of the easiest ways to identify that pattern is to focus on the major challenges Jesus issued to His followers as He developed them: "come and you will see" (John 1:39), "follow me" (John 1:43), "follow me and I will send you out to fish for people" (Matthew 4:19), and "go and bear fruit" (John 15:16). I call this model "4 Chair Discipling." It is a simple and highly transferable model that helpfully depicts the development of a disciple from before he or she meets Christ until the point when they themselves become a multiplying disciple-maker who is bearing much fruit.

As we begin this journey into looking into the model Jesus gave us, there are a couple of things that we need to keep in mind.

First, the command given in Matthew 28 is to "make disciples of all nations." This literally means to make disciples who can make disciples. Our command is not discipleship but disciple-making. Discipleship normally refers to what you do with Christians. The term "discipleship" makes most people think of deeper Bible studies or weightier content for Christians. This is important, but it isn't our mandate. Our mandate is disciple-making, which is the whole process from unbeliever to fully-trained, reproducing disciple-maker.

Second, the genius of Jesus, in my mind, is that He recognized that people were at different stages in the disciple-making journey, and that was okay. He started where people were and intentionally moved them to a deeper level of growth and maturity. He started with seekers (Chair 1) and then moved them to believers (Chair 2). In time, He challenged these believers to become workers in the harvest field (Chair 3) and, finally, fully trained reproducing disciple-makers (Chair 4). With this in mind, let's begin to look at the four challenges of Jesus represented by these four chairs.

CHALLENGE 1: COME AND SEE (JOHN 1:39)

This first challenge is given in John 1:35–39. It is the invitation to Andrew and John (who is assumed to be the second disciple) to "come and see." This challenge gives us insight into how Jesus developed His initial relationships with several of His early disciples. Andrew and

John were spiritual seekers who were engaged with the ministry of John the Baptist, who preached that the Messiah was coming after him. In fact, John had just identified Jesus as the Lamb of God. So the two men began to follow Jesus as He taught. When He saw them following Him, Jesus asked them a simple question: "What do you want?"

"Where are You staying?" they asked.

Jesus replied, "Come and you will see."

The Greek word translated "come" literally means "just show up." This is a critical first step for seekers to take. They must be willing to just show up in order to learn more. Andrew and John were obviously spiritual seekers who were engaged with John the Baptist. They were curious about the one John had identified as the Lamb of God! Jesus sensed their seeking heart, and responded by giving them a gift of His time. John gives us an interesting detail by telling us that this conversation took place around the tenth hour (4 p.m.) and that He spent the day with them. The Jewish day ended at sunset, which means that Jesus spent a minimum of two hours with Andrew and John.

What do you suppose they talked about for those two hours? Like most Jewish people of that day, Andrew and John wondered who the Messiah would be and when, where, and how He would come. Perhaps the conversation went like this:

"Tell me guys," Jesus began, "what do you know about the coming Messiah?" Jesus was a good rabbi who loved to help people learn by asking questions.

"Well, we know He is going to be born in Bethlehem," Andrew replied, "for Micah 5:2 tells us that 'out of Bethlehem . . . will come for me one who will be ruler over Israel.'"

"Wouldn't it be nice to be born in the Messiah's hometown?" John added. "I wish I would have been born in Bethlehem!"

"That would be exciting, wouldn't it?" Jesus said. "By the way, did you know I was born in Bethlehem? When my mother was pregnant with me, Caesar Augustus issued a degree that everyone had to return to their hometown to register, and since my parents were from the line of David, we returned to Bethlehem. It was during that time I was born in Bethlehem."

"I thought You were born in Galilee. What an amazing privilege to be born in the same village that the Messiah is coming from!"

"Yes it is!" Jesus smiled. "Tell me, what else do you know about the coming Messiah?"

"The rabbis don't understand this," Andrew said, "but we are told that the Messiah will come out of Egypt, as it says in Hosea 11:1: 'Out of Egypt I called my Son.' How can you be born in Bethlehem, yet come out of Egypt?"

"Yes, that does seem like a problem," Jesus said. "Do you think it could have happened this way? I was born in Bethlehem around the time Herod the Great killed all the male babies. An angel appeared to my stepfather, Joseph, and told us to flee, and we fled to Egypt, where we lived for a few years. After a few years, an angel told my stepfather it was safe to return. We wanted to settle in Bethlehem, but the angel instructed my parents to settle in Nazareth. So my situation is just like that. I was born in Bethlehem, yet I was called out of Egypt."

"Yeah, that makes a lot of sense," John replied. "I'm going to share that with my rabbi."

About then Andrew was struck with a realization. "Wait a minute," he said. "You're not hinting that You might be the Messiah, are You? You are from Nazareth—and nothing good can come out of Nazareth, can it?"

Again Jesus smiled and said, "Is that right? Look again at Isaiah 11:1. Isaiah tells us in this Messianic passage that 'a shoot (*netzer*) will come up from the stump of Jesse.' The town named Nazareth alludes to the royal descent of Jesus as the Natzorean ("branch") from the stump of Jesse. Some people call Nazareth 'shoot town.'"[1] Jesus paused. "I am from 'shoot town.' In fact, I am that 'branch' from the stump of Jesse, the original Natzorean, the one from Nazareth! I am the Messiah. I was born in Bethlehem, came out of Egypt, and am the branch from 'shoot town!'"

This is a fictional conversation, of course, but it is based on three passages of Scripture Matthew references in his gospel (Matthew 2:1, 15, 23). It is clear that a conversation like this took place, because Andrew bursts out of his first meeting with Jesus and proclaims, "We have found the Messiah" (John 1:41). Can you hear the excitement in his voice? Isn't this what happens when seekers find the Savior they are looking for?

When relating to these religious seekers, Jesus did what He did with a couple of His disciples on the Emmaus road in Luke 24. He opened the Scriptures (24:32), explained to them what the Scriptures said about Himself (24:27), and then allowed the Holy Spirit to open their minds to the truth (24:45).

Spending time with seekers and inviting them to "come and see" is the first step in making disciples. It's a step that is easy to duplicate. After spending time with Jesus Himself, Philip invites Nathaneal to come and see (John 1:46). The Samaritan woman with whom Jesus had conversation at a well returned to her village and invited everyone in it, "Come, see a man who told me everything I ever did. Could this be the Messiah?" (John 4:29).

In the book of Acts, the apostles took the Gospel first to the Jews and later to the Gentiles, focusing their attention on those who were curious and were investigating spiritual things. From preaching at Pentecost (Acts 2:5–36) to the Ethiopian eunuch (Acts 8:26–39), this pattern was observed. Paul found the responsive seekers in the synagogues (Acts 13:14–44; 14:1; 17:1–3; 18:1–4; and 19:8). Paul also sought out the responsive Gentiles and met them at their point of interest (Acts 16:13–15; 17:22–34; 19:9–10). This simple challenge to "come and see" was built upon the premise that the Father through the Holy Spirit is drawing people to Himself (John 6:44), and our job is to simply discern who these people are and be ready to provide an answer to them why Jesus is the Savior (1 Peter 3:15). It is not a difficult first step. It simply requires us to be willing to be used by God to give the gift of time and show the love of Christ to those who are seeking God.

CHALLENGE 2: FOLLOW ME (JOHN 1:43)

The second challenge, represented by Chair 2, was given to many in various ways. We see it first in John 1:43, where we are told that Jesus "decided to leave for Galilee. Finding Philip, he said to him, 'Follow me.'" This second challenge moves the seeker in Chair 1 to the status of a believer. It implies that a person has made a decision about Christ. An inner transformation has taken place. A seeker has been moved by the Holy Spirit to "repent and believe" and had decided to trust Jesus for salvation. Now they are ready to take the next step. The second challenge is, "Follow me."

Throughout the disciples' journey, Jesus challenges them to "follow me" as a reminder of their primary responsibility. At the beginning of their relationship, Jesus tells Matthew the tax collector, "Follow me," and "Matthew got up and followed him" (Matthew 9:9). Later Jesus drew His disciples into a deeper commitment when He said "follow me" and I will make you fishers of men (Matthew 4:19). In Matthew 10:38 Jesus makes it clear what's at stake for those who waver in following Him. "Whoever does not take up their cross and follow me," Jesus says, "is not worthy of me." Following is the mark of a true believer in John 10:27, where Jesus says, "My sheep listen to my voice; I know them, and they follow me." Even at the end of His ministry, Jesus returns to a discouraged Peter who had denied Him three times and says, "Follow me" (John 21:19, 22).

This word translated "follow" is the Greek word *akoloutheo*, and it literally means to come behind, to follow in my steps, to learn of me, to join me in the journey as a disciple.

It was my job, as a young boy of eight years old on our South Dakota farm, to milk our two cows every morning. We affectionately called them Betsy and Beulah. On those mornings when we woke up to two or three feet of fresh snow, my dad would put on his overshoes and cut a path in front of me to the barn where the Betsy and Beulah stayed. As he broke a path for me in the snow, he would say, "Follow me." I simply walked behind him, placing my feet in the steps he laid ahead of me. This is a vivid illustration of Jesus's challenge. "Come," Jesus says, "learn of Me. Follow in My steps."

"Come and see" assumes curiosity. "Follow me" assumes commitment. This challenge is a call to a deeper level of the discipling journey than just "come and see." It assumes a desire to learn from the rabbi. It demands a learning process of walking in the steps of the master. It paints a picture of becoming like the one we are following, allowing

Him to lead us. It demands that we walk as He walked, love as He loves, do what He did, serve as He served. It is a challenge to be a learner, which is what the word "disciple" (*mathetes*) literally means.

This is a common challenge in disciple-making throughout the New Testament. Paul picked up on this challenge in 1 Corinthians 11:1, where he instructs his readers, "Follow my example as I follow the example of Christ." The Greek word Paul uses that is translated "follow" is the word *mimethes*, from which we derive the words "mimic" and "imitate." In other words, Paul is saying, "As I follow Christ, imitate my life and you too will learn of Him." It is a challenge we should be able to extend to others as we mature in Him.

John 3:22 tells us Jesus spent time with His disciples. If the disciples were going to imitate Him, He had to give them time to get to know Him. Jesus knew that life change comes through relationships. And relationships cannot be rushed. So Jesus took His disciples with Him to a wedding party (John 2:2), and on a journey, along with His mother and brothers, to the city of Capernaum for a couple of days (John 2:12). He then took them to an important religious service (Passover, John 2:13), to some meetings with religious leaders (John 3), out into the Judean countryside (John 3:22), into some potential family conflicts (John 3:20), and on a short-term missions trip (John 4:4). These early followers learned from Jesus as they followed Him.

"Follow me" is a practical and simple step any of us can take as we make disciples. It requires us to invite people into our lives and spend time with them, allowing them a chance to get to know us and for us to get to know them. It simply requires loving people as we love God.

CHALLENGE 3: FOLLOW ME AND I WILL MAKE YOU FISHERS OF MEN (MATTHEW 4:19 ESV)

The third challenge is a summons to leave the comfort of Chair 2 and move into Chair 3. Two parallel passages of Scripture, Matthew 4:18–22 and Mark 1:16–20, help us understand this critical challenge from the heart of our Master Disciple-Maker.[2] This third challenge, "Follow Me, and I will make you fishers of men," is one of the most misunderstood and least lived-out of the teachings of Jesus.

It comes as a surprise to many people to learn that the events recorded in Mark 1:16–20 took place at least eighteen months into Jesus's ministry. In these verses, Jesus is passing along the Sea of Galilee when He calls to Simon (Peter) and Andrew, "Follow me, and I will make you fishers of men." Contrary to popular belief, this is not the first time Jesus encounters these men. They had been following Jesus for several months. But in this episode, Jesus challenges them to go deeper. They move from simply following Him to becoming His ministry team. Four individuals are involved in this challenge. They are James and John and Simon and Andrew. Later Matthew will be added to this team.

This third challenge by Jesus is loaded with meaning. It is clearly strategic.[3] First and foremost, the challenge is relational. As in the previous challenge, Jesus invites the disciples to "come and follow me." But from this point forward, Jesus is going to make an even greater investment of time in these men, who will later become a part of His twelve apostles. These are not the Twelve yet—they are simply what I call His ministry team: a team of faithful followers that He is going to take deeper.

Second, this challenge is clearly intentional. Jesus clearly says, "I *will* make you." He had a clear goal and a clear plan for developing His disciples as reproducing disciple-makers. Immediately after challenging these disciples to become fishers of men, Jesus led them on six "fishing trips" to give them confidence in sharing their faith.[4] Shortly thereafter he led them intentionally on four additional mission trips, which extended over several days. He was intentional about developing His disciples as "fishers of men," teaching them to reproduce their lives in others.

Mark 1:21–2:17 clearly lays out these evangelistic fishing trips. First Jesus takes the disciples to a synagogue where they watch Him cast out a demon in the presence of a religious unsaved crowd (Mark 1:21–28). He then leads them to Peter's home where He heals Peter's mother-in-law (family ministry, Mark 1:29–31). Next Jesus preaches to the crowds in Peter's hometown of Capernaum (neighborhood ministry, Mark 1:32–34). Each step of the way, the disciples are learning new principles for sharing their faith as they watch Jesus.

After a late evening of ministry, early the next morning Jesus arises to get His marching orders for the day by slipping away to pray. The disciples search everywhere for Him. Indeed the whole city was looking for Him (Mark 1:37). In the eyes of the disciples, I'm sure what Jesus did next must have seemed foolish—He turned His back on the crowds and said, "we must go to the other cities and towns . . . that is why I have come." What a moment this must have been for His disciples as they watched Jesus intentionally stay focused on His priorities. He was helping them understand what it means to be fishers of men rather than crowd pleasers consumed with the demands of the multitudes.

After these initial fishing trips, Jesus changes gears and takes His disciples on what I like to call His second missions trip. This trip probably lasted several weeks (Josephus tells us there were at least 204 villages in Galilee large enough to have synagogues), as they traveled to all the area synagogues "preaching and driving out demons" (Mark 1:39). I can imagine Jesus allowing the disciples to share in the reading of the Scriptures and testifying about who the Messiah was as they traveled to the synagogues. This time Jesus gave them repeated examples of fishing for men so they could learn to do it themselves and not just be "amazed" (Mark 1:27).

From here in the Gospel of Mark we find Jesus reaching out to the leper—the unlovely of the community (Mark 1:40–45). On this fishing trip, Jesus was clearly shaping the disciples' values. He was teaching them that it is not always the people who look just like us about whom we should be concerned. They were beginning to observe that there were many seekers among the unlovely that needed the touch of the Master.

Next, in Mark 2:1–2, Jesus invites many of the religious leaders and teachers of the law to a home, where they are seated inside while the crowds gather outside. A group of men, deeply concerned for their friend, go to great trouble and expense to get their friend close to Jesus. They lower him through the roof after tearing it apart. "When

Jesus saw their faith," He healed the man. This experience taught the disciples that faith is visible and can be demonstrated by actions.

On the sixth "fishing trip" Jesus does the unthinkable—He invites a "tax collector" to join them (Mark 2:13–20). This pushes the disciples well outside of their comfort zone, especially when Matthew throws an evangelistic party with all his tax collector and "sinner" friends. I can just imagine how uncomfortable the disciples were, hoping that none of their good Jewish friends would see whom they were eating with. Jesus was clearly intentional in making His disciples fishers of men!

Not only was this third challenge relational and intentional, but it was also missional. Jesus clearly knew His mission was to leave behind a movement of disciples capable of reproducing disciples themselves. "I will make you *fishers of men.*"

Jesus was calling His disciples to recognize that, when they were fully trained, they would repeat this same disciple-making process in the lives of others. Right before He ascended into heaven, Jesus repeated this charge to them in the Great Commission.

While Jesus's personal mission was to die on the cross for the sins of the world, His ministry calling was to advance His Father's Kingdom agenda by initiating a movement of multiplying disciples. This movement would become the Church, which eventually spread from Jerusalem to Judea and to the uttermost parts of the world, so that one day, "a great multitude that no one could count, from every nation, tribe, people and language" will stand before the throne proclaiming, "Salvation belongs to our God, who sits on the throne, and to the Lamb" (Revelation 7:9–10).

In other words, Jesus's mission was not to reach the world but to make disciples who were capable of reaching the world. Jesus knew that if He made disciple-makers, 2,000 years later there would be over a billion Christ-followers through the law of multiplication. If He had reached the world of His day—an estimated 250 million people—but had not trained them to multiply, we would not be here today. The movement would have ended after the first generation. But by training His disciples how to multiply themselves, hundreds of millions of people are following Christ today.

This level of disciple-making is more demanding, but the rewards are exhilarating! Fewer make it to this level because of the intentionality it requires (Matthew 10:37); but when they do, the impact is multiplied. The workers are few, but the harvest remains plentiful.

CHALLENGE 4: GO AND BEAR FRUIT (JOHN 15:16)

Right at the end of Jesus's ministry, Jesus had just finished His last Passover meal with His disciples in the Upper Room. They sang a hymn and then made their way to the Garden of Gethsemane where Jesus would be betrayed.[5] On the way, Jesus stopped in a vineyard and delivered His famous teaching about the vine and the branches (John 15:1–11). During this final lesson before His arrest, Jesus makes a couple of very profound statements.

First, Jesus calls His disciples "friends." Throughout the book of John, Jesus's descriptions of His disciples become increasingly intimate. In John 1, they are called seekers. In John 2:11, they are identified as disciples. By John 13:13, Jesus calls them servants or coworkers. But now, Jesus says, "I no longer call you servants, because a servant does not know his master's business. Instead, I have called you friends, for everything that I learned from my Father I have made known to you" (John 15:15).

Jesus moves His disciples to a whole new level of relationship with Him, from Chair 3 to Chair 4. And the reason for this is clear. He will be going away soon, and they must "go and bear fruit" (John 15:16). Jesus is now saying, "As the Father has sent me, I am sending you" (John 20:21).

The challenge here is similar to what Jesus will command His disciples in the Great Commission. They are to go and do what He did. They are to repeat the process in others. *I have shown you, now go and do likewise. Go, make disciples of all nations, doing what I have done with you.* This challenge is not easy, but it is simple. Fruit bearing requires that we "abide" in the Vine (Jesus) and allow the Vine to produce fruit through us. Our task is abiding. His task is bearing fruit. We will bear fruit to the degree that we abide in Him and walk as He walked.

Jesus recognized that people were at different stages in the disciple-making journey. He started where people were and intentionally moved them to a deeper level of growth and maturity. His desired end product was always fruit, and fruit was always a metaphor for multiplication. He knew He could not work this process with everyone, so He had to choose a few who would repeat the process. Jesus masterfully challenged these "uneducated and ordinary" men to become a major force in advancing His Kingdom. He wants to do the same in our lives and teach us to repeat the process with others.

PONDERINGS

1. What is your initial reaction to the concept of "4 Chair Discipling"? Be specific.

_____

_____

2. Take a few moments to read Mark 1:21–2:17. Do you see the six fishing trips identified in this chapter? How do these fishing trips relate to the challenge Jesus issues His disciples to "Follow me and I will make you fishers of men"?

_____

_____

3. In which of the four chairs do you think you are currently sitting? From what you know now, what do you think is your next step?

_____

_____

Visit www.4ChairDiscipling.com for more resources.

CHAPTER FIVE

Chair 1: The Lost

For almost twenty years, I considered myself a very religious person. I attended Mass regularly, came from a family that prayed the rosary together on our knees, and even served as an altar boy for the priest. During the summer, we attended vacation religious classes, memorized the questions from the catechism, and were active in church services. Open to God but far from Him. Active in religion but spiritually dead. On several occasions I tried to read the family Bible but found it meaningless, just black words printed on a white page.

Romans 6:23 tells us that "the wages of sin is death." I was a sinner by birth and by choice, and that meant I was spiritually dead. Now, if you had showed me that verse in those days, I may have agreed with you outwardly. But inwardly I would have felt that I was better than most people because I attended religious services and stayed busy in church activities. For all my busyness, I was spiritually dead. And spiritually dead are incapable of doing anything.

It's easy to believe that a lost person who doesn't know Jesus is very much alive. They may even be religious. If so, we can convince ourselves that they just need a little more church, or a little more Bible, or a little more faith. We can convince ourselves that they just need to make Jesus a bigger part of their life. But the fact is, instead of turning over a new leaf, what they really need is a new life. If we agree with Paul's assessment of our situation in Ephesians 2—"As for you, you were dead in your transgressions and sins"—then we have to accept the remedy he prescribes: "But because of his great love for us, God, who is rich in mercy, made us alive with Christ" (Ephesians 2:4–5). The lost don't need to be rehabilitated. They need to be resurrected.

The people who sit in Chair 1 are not simply nice people who need a little more life; they are spiritually dead people who are incapable of knowing God through their own efforts. The lost in Chair 1 are lying in a spiritual coffin and incapable of coming to life on their own. The Bible has much more to say about people like this, and it is not all that pleasant. According to the Scriptures, they "follow the ways of this world" and belong to the "ruler of the kingdom of the air" (Ephesians 2:2). "By nature" they are "deserving of wrath (Ephesians 2:3). The person in Chair 1 is "hostile to God," "does not submit to God," and is completely unable to do so (Romans 8:7). In fact, that person is "an enemy of God" and therefore "cannot please God," no matter how hard they try (Romans 5:10; 8:8). When they are physically dead, they are destined to eternity apart from God (Luke 16:23; Revelation 20:15; John 3:16).

I wish I didn't have to make these seemingly harsh statements. But this is the clear teaching of God's Word. And until we come to terms with how the Bible describes our true condition before we come to Christ, the true condition of those who haven't been saved by Christ's sacrifice, we cannot help ourselves or anyone else. Truth can hurt. But it also brings true healing. The journey of becoming a true disciple of Christ begins with an honest appreciation of our life without Christ. We are dead. Lost. Alone. Unable to save ourselves.

The good news is that Christ can reverse this condition. As the late Howard Hendricks explained in one of his last sermons, "The amazing thing, my friend, is not that you die, but the amazing thing is that you live. [We] think we are in the land of the living on the way to the land of dying. My friend, nothing could be further from the biblical truth. You and I are in the land of dying and on our way to the land of the living."[1]

THE PROCESS MODELED

God is a missionary God. Beginning in the Old Testament, God blessed Abraham to be a blessing to all the nations of the earth. "I will make you into a great nation, and I will bless you; I will make your name great, and you will be a blessing. I will bless those who bless you, and whoever curses you I will curse; and all peoples on earth will be blessed through you" (Genesis 12:2–3). Continuing into the New Testament, God sent His Son to be a missionary to us. As that perfect missionary, living a perfect life on mission, Jesus modeled how to make an impact. He modeled what it means to be "sent" and to live life on mission. Jesus demonstrated perfectly the process of finding lost people and challenging them to move forward in the disciple-making process. Let's begin by looking closely into the process Jesus modeled.

He left the comforts of His heavenly home and entered into our world. God became flesh and dwelt among us in Jesus. Jesus left the comforts of His eternal home and, by adding humanity to His deity, came into our world. He became like us. He identified with our joys and sorrows, our fears and concerns. He did not come as the royalty that He was. Instead He became like us in every way. He did not rent a large synagogue, hold large meetings, and demand that people come to pay tribute to Him. On the contrary, He came to us as a babe in a manger, to serve and not be served. Ultimately He became known as a "friend of sinners."

He prepared Himself, learning the context and culture in which He was sent. Jesus spent thirty years in preparation. He learned obedience, studied the Scriptures, and prepared Himself through what He learned as He went about His everyday life. Most of His life was spent in obscurity. We call these the silent years. Yet for Jesus it was a life of learning to cope with the challenges of everyday living. He lived as a child, a friend, a son, a provider, and a business-man much longer than He lived in the limelight as the controversial

Messiah. He came into our context and modeled life as God intended it to be lived. The first challenge he extended to the initial disciples, to "come and see," was a challenge simply to observe how He lived as the perfect human, the second Adam. To come and see the simple patterns of His balanced lifestyle, perfected in the context of the world in which He had been called.

He made Himself available and intentionally developed relationships. Imagine the day, after thirty years of relative obscurity, that the Father tells Jesus, "Today is the day. Go and be baptized by Your cousin John." Imagine the thoughts that occupied Him as He made the eighty-mile trek to Bethany. Did He know what was ahead? Did He know His life as a businessman was over?[2] Did He anticipate the Holy Spirit's anointing at His baptism? This we know for sure: Jesus made Himself available. He lived a perfectly dependent lifestyle. When the Father said, "Go!" Jesus responded in obedience.

At His baptism, the Spirit came upon Him, and after forty days of fasting and prayer, Jesus returned to where His cousin John was baptizing and made Himself available to be used by His heavenly Father. He began to participate in the ministry John had prepared. Jesus began identifying those whom the Father was drawing to Him. Called to disciple-making, He now spent hours with Andrew and John, Philip and Nathaneal (John 1:39, 43). He made a trip to Cana with His disciples, where He performed His first miracle (John 2:1). He then spent a few days in Capernaum, with His disciples and family members, no doubt answering questions about this miracle (John 2:12). After the Passover in Jerusalem, He met Nicodemus late at night to answer his questions (John 3). He spent several days traveling through Samaria, addressing the spiritual questions of seeking people (John 4). In short, He made Himself fully available to invest in seekers who were looking for answers.

He responded to those who showed interest. When Jesus began His ministry, He simply responded to those who were seeking by asking them, "What do you want?" (John 1:38). Jesus knew no one could come to Him "unless the Father draws him," so He kept His eyes open for those who showed signs of being drawn to the Father. When

He saw interest, he made Himself available to their needs and questions. Throughout His ministry, Jesus built a multitude of relationships and watched for those who showed interest, knowing that the Father was drawing people to Himself. In this way, Jesus worked in partnership with the Holy Spirit, because He knew the Holy Spirit was doing His job of convicting the world of guilt . . . and sin (John 16:8, 9). Jesus came to seek and save that which was lost, and He did this by partnering with the Holy Spirit and responding to those who showed interest.

Jesus challenged seekers to repent and believe. Like John the Baptist before Him, Jesus preached a simple message: "Repent, for the kingdom of heaven has come near" (Matthew 3:2; 4:17). He knew His listeners were dead in their sin and that unless one is born again he will never be able to "see" or "enter" the Kingdom of God (John 3:3, 5). Dead people cannot see or walk. They need the life that comes from above. That life comes through repentance. Jesus boldly proclaimed that message of repentance and belief.

THE NEEDS OF SEEKERS

The person in Chair 1, the person without Christ, has many needs. The pattern of Christ's life clearly models the best way to meet these needs.

First and foremost, Chair 1 people need Christ-followers in their lives who are willing to enter into their world relationally. This is what Jesus did for us. He left the comfort and glory of heaven and became like us in every way. He went where His people were so He could identify with them and so they in turn could get to know Him. Moved with Great Commandment love, Jesus so loved the world that He laid down His life for us.

Who has God placed right around you? Are you entering into their world? Would people identify you as a "friend of sinners," as Jesus was? Are you willing to leave the comfort of your home or church to enter into the world of those without Christ? For years I had taught that we need to "walk as Jesus walked" and to "do what Jesus did" (1 John 2:6; John 14:12). Then one day I asked myself, in an exercise of personal reflection, how many non-Christians would call me their best friend.

And to be honest, I couldn't name any! I had become so consumed with Christians that I no longer had friendships with non-Christians. Oh, I knew some unbelievers, and I even waved to them on the way to church. But good friendships—I didn't have any. I was no longer walking as Jesus walked.

This had to change! It was on that day that I began a fifteen-year journey of praying for my neighbors, reaching out to them, building redemptive relationships, and making them my priority. God honored that intentionality, as yearly we saw some of our neighbors trust Christ.

My wife, Char, and I recently moved to Louisville, Kentucky. Our new neighborhood prides itself on being independent, and many of our neighbors seem uninterested in developing new friendships. I knew right away this would make it a challenge to reach them with the Gospel. I found myself asking, "How would Jesus respond?"

Neil was the exception. Neil seemed open to talking, as long as we talked about what he loved. And he loved guns. He had several dozen guns in his home and belonged to several gun clubs and shooting ranges. I had grown up with guns on our farm in South Dakota. But after living in a suburb of Chicago for more than thirty years, I had almost forgotten what a gun looked like. So I decided to enter into Neil's world. Would he teach me what he knew? Would he show me how to shoot again? Would he take me to the shooting range?

Neil welcomed the challenge and I entered into his world. Through our newfound hobby, Neil and I have become good friends. He recently attended an activity at our church. It was one of just a few times he had been to church in the last thirty years. Our friendship is growing.

Chair 1 people need friends who will enter into their world.

Second, Chair 1 people need Christ-followers who have prepared themselves. Jesus understood the culture and context in which He ministered because He lived among the people for thirty years. He was prepared for the questions, because He became a student of His culture. He was prepared with answers to the issues facing the people of His day. What are the unique questions seekers are asking in your neighborhood and workplace? How has the Father prepared you to answer those questions? God has helped you endure challenges in your life. You did not face these challenges by coincidence. Perhaps God wants to use you to help others who face similar problems. What needs are your neighbors facing that no one is addressing?

I will never forget Scott. He was one of the most interesting seekers I have ever met. Scott was a scientist. When he first came to my Bible study, he asked few questions, but I saw him taking a lot of notes. One day he asked if he could meet with me alone. When Scott showed up, he had a yellow pad filled with more than fifty questions about God and the Bible. He had questions from Genesis to Revelation. One by one, I tried to answer them. If I could answer a question satisfactorily, he'd check it off. If I didn't know the answer, I told him I'd try to get back to him. This continued for four meetings, each with dozens of questions on a yellow pad.

At our fifth meeting, Scott simply folded up his yellow pad and said, "I'm ready."

"Ready for what?"

"I'm ready to trust Christ for His salvation. You've answered my questions, so now I'm ready."

I questioned him, and it was clear he fully understood his decision. I asked him if he wanted me to lead him in a prayer of faith. "No," he said. "My wife has been praying for me, and I want to accept Christ with her. It will mean a lot to her."

I smiled and told him to drive carefully on the way home. He understood what I meant! Later that day he called to tell me how thankful he was that I took time to answer his questions. God had uniquely prepared me for Scott and Scott for me. It was my joy. Chair 1 people need Christ-followers who have prepared themselves as well as they can and are willing to answer difficult questions.

Third, Chair 1 people need Christ followers who make themselves available and will invest in friendships. Jesus made Himself available— when the Father said, "go and be baptized" and when Andrew asked, "Where are You staying?" Jesus was never in a rush; He lived fully on mission. He saw people's interruptions as opportunities for ministry.

A couple of weeks ago, my neighbor, Neil, asked if I would ride with him out of town to look at a gun shop with him. The drive was two and a half hours one way. My schedule was packed, but this was a great opportunity to spend some time with him. I knew it meant at least five hours in a car talking, so I made myself available.

On the way home, Neil dropped a surprise in my lap. In the course of our conversation, I thanked him for spending time with me, teaching me what he knew about guns. "You ask good questions," he said, "and you listen well. I have enjoyed it." Then he continued, "Do you mind if I ask you a question?"

"No of course not," I responded.

"Do you know what a born-again Christian is?" he asked. "My best friend who lives out of state told me he has become one, and I'm wondering what that means."

We spent over an hour talking about what a born-again Christian is. I'm sure Neil's friend has been praying for him. I'm glad I made myself available that day. I'm excited to see what God is going to do in that friendship. Chair 1 people need Christian friends who will make themselves available and invest time with them.

Finally, Chair 1 people need someone to present the Gospel clearly to them. I remember the very first time I heard and understood the good news of the salvation Christ offers. I quickly embraced it and was eager to tell others this good news. For years I wondered why no one had told me sooner. What could my life have been like if I had made this decision earlier?

All around us, people are searching for this good news. God's Spirit is drawing people to Himself. The Holy Spirit is doing His job. God Word is true, "the harvest is plentiful, but the workers are few" (Matthew 9:37). We must do our job, too, and with boldness and clarity, like Jesus and John the Baptist, proclaim clearly that "the Kingdom is near" and that repentance is the key that unlocks the door to a relationship with Christ. If we don't tell our friends, who will?

Emir had attended my executive study for several months. Clearly one morning, while I was praying for my study, the Lord impressed upon my heart that I needed to clearly present the Gospel to Emir. I was nervous. I wasn't sure if I would do it well.

I met Emir for breakfast, and I pulled out a "Knowing God Personally" tract, and asked Emir if I could share it with him.[3] After walking through it, Emir thanked me, and we finished our breakfast. I felt like a failure and sensed that I hadn't presented the Gospel very well.

On the way to work that morning, Emir pulled off to the side of the road and prayed to trust Christ. He called me later that day and thanked me. The Holy Spirit had succeeded where I felt I was unclear. God delights in using even the most lowly among us to share His good news. Emir is now walking with God and has seen His family respond to God's good news also. Chair 1 people need Christ-followers who will clearly present to them the good news of God's saving grace.

PRINCIPLES FOR MINISTRY TO PEOPLE IN CHAIR 1

Countless books have been written about evangelism to the lost. Here are a few principles I find helpful for reaching out to those in Chair 1.

1) The challenge to "come and see" is a simple challenge. It doesn't demand a lot from either the person giving the challenge or the one receiving it. It is a beginning step, and it's easy to reproduce. Jesus invited His disciples to "come and see" (John 1:46). After Jesus spoke to the Samaritan woman at the well, she ran back to her village and called her neighbors to "come and see" (John 4:29). What does this challenge look like in practical terms? "Come and see" can mean a simple invitation to dinner in your home. It can be a simple invitation to attend an outreach event or church service, or a simple golf outing to deepen a relationship. "Come and see" invites people into our lives to go deeper in friendship.

2) Outreach is a process. Many Chair 1 people will need to hear the good news several times before they are ready to receive it. Few respond to the Gospel the first time it is shared. Isaiah 28:23–29 visualizes this in a natural, organic way. I call this process "Spiritual CPR," a helpful shorthand for the process of outreach. Physical CPR is the resuscitation of physical life, but spiritual CPR is bringing people to real, spiritual life.

"C" stands for Cultivation. Cultivation is breaking up hard ground so that it can receive the seed. Isaiah visualizes this by asking the rhetorical question, "When a farmer plows for planting, does he plow continually? Does he keep on breaking up and working the soil?" (28:24). Breaking up the hardened ground is the hardest part of the process. Farmers fully understand this. It is when the farm tractor works the hardest. The ground needs to be plowed, disked, and then cultivated; all to break up the hardened ground to make it ready to receive the seed.

Often the hardest part of evangelism is this process of building friendships with the lost so they will be receptive to the seed of the Gospel (see John 4:38). If we fail to do this hard part, most of our seed-sowing will fall on hard soil and be unproductive (see Mark 4:15). This is the crucial first step, but Isaiah reminds us it is only a preliminary step.

Next comes planting. The "P" in CPR stands for Planting. Planting is sowing the seed at the right time, the right depth, and in the right way (Isaiah 28:25–26). Earlier in Isaiah, the prophet identifies five different types of plants, and the seeds of each plant must be planted in a different way at a different time and a different depth. In the same way, planting in a relationship means sowing the seed into the friendship with a lost person. There is no magic formula for how best to do this. Fortunately "God instructs us and teaches him the right way" (Isaiah 28:26).

"R" stands for Reaping, harvesting the crop at the right time. Spiritual harvest requires sharing the Good News, clearly and concisely, and calling for a response. It is bringing in the harvest.

Every farmer knows that you don't plant before you cultivate, and you don't expect to reap before you sow. Outreach is a process. And not all of us participate in the same step in the process. Some sow and some reap. Regardless of our role with a particular person, we rejoice together as God uses different people for different parts of His CPR process.

3) Jesus Christ is the only means by which a person can be restored in his or her relationship to God. Jesus is not the best way. He is the only way! There is no other way to have our sins forgiven.

No other way to find eternal life. Only Jesus conquered death and rose from the grave. And only Jesus can give the life our friends so desperately need. This truth alone should transform us as we begin, like Jesus, to see people without Him as eternally lost.

4) Evangelism is most effective when we are motivated by love. For the apostle Paul, as for Jesus, love for God and for people was the motivation for his evangelism. Paul said he was "constrained by the love of God." Our love for God is deepened as we understand what great things God has done for us (Mark 5:19a). God has made us "children of God" (John 1:12), granted us eternal life (John 3:16), made us each a "new creation" (Galatians 2:20), and delivered us "from the dominion of darkness" and has forgiven us completely of our sins (Colossians 1:13–14). In light of all this, we should be overwhelmed by God's goodness toward us, "overflowing with thankfulness," as Paul says (Colossians 2:7b). The more we grasp all that God has done for us, the more our love of God compels us to share the Good News with others.

Furthermore, love is developed as we understand how the Lord has shown mercy to us (Mark 5:19b). Seven times in Scripture Jesus looks upon the people and is "moved with compassion." Christ's compassion stemmed from a clear understanding of the reality of hell. Luke 16 clearly portrays the consequence of humankind apart from Christ. Those consequences are eternal and agonizing. Love compels us to share with the lost the truth about Christ.

5) Evangelism is a byproduct of a healthy body. Healthy things reproduce. As individual Christians live holy lives, they reach people for Christ. "Create in me a clean heart, Oh God; and renew a right spirit within me," David prayed. "*Then* will I teach transgressors thy ways and sinners shall be converted unto thee" (Psalm 51:10, 13 KJV, italics added). Similarly, churches that are healthy—that are made up of individual Christians living holy lives—tend to be communities that draw people to Christ. When God draws people to Himself, He often draws them into churches that are healthy enough to care for new spiritual babies. In other words, internal health tends to produce external multiplication. Acts tells us that the very first Christian community constantly devoted themselves "to the apostles' teaching and to fellowship, to the breaking of bread and to prayer," and as a result, "the Lord added to their number daily those who were being saved" (Acts 2:42, 47).

6) Evangelism is best achieved through relationships. Tom was a neighbor who became a good friend. When our neighborhood organized a softball team and played in a league together, it provided a great opportunity for me to connect with non-Christian neighbors and initiate new friendships. Tom was one of those friends. As our friendship developed, I had a chance to share my story of faith. When I asked Tom if he wanted to learn more about my faith, he pulled back. He wasn't ready and a wall went up between us immediately. I backed off, but I kept praying for Tom. Our friendship continued, but I could tell Tom had put up a protective wall.

Several months went by and I didn't hear from Tom. Then late one night the doorbell rang. *Who could this be at such a late hour?* I wondered. When I opened the door, there was Tom.

"Can we talk?" His face was full of concern. "My wife just served me divorce papers," he said. "I had no idea this was coming."

After a couple of gut-wrenching hours of conversation, I had another chance to share with Tom my story and God's Story. Tom was receptive this time and put his faith in Christ. His wife still divorced him, but Tom is growing in the Lord and has told me on a number of occasions how grateful he is that I shared the Gospel with him. I am so grateful I had built that friendship with Tom. I've often wondered where Tom would be today, if we didn't have that friendship.

7) We reap in proportion to what we sow. God's job is to prepare people's hearts and to draw them to Himself (John 6). The Holy Spirit's role is to convict the world of sin (John 16:8). Our job is to find those people God has already prepared and to proclaim the truth to them. Our job is to cultivate, plant, and pray for the harvest. Our reaping will be proportional to our sowing. Those who plant abundantly will reap abundantly, but those who plant little will reap little.

The goal of our mission to those in Chair 1 is to help them move to Chair 2. Join me in the next chapter to learn about this next step in the process of disciple-making.

PONDERINGS

1. What aspect of Chair 1 discipling is the easiest for you to wrap your arms around?

_____

_____

_____

2. What aspect of Chair 1 discipling do you find the most intimidating?

_____

_____

_____

3. Take a few minutes to identify people in your life who dwell in Chair 1. What steps can you take to deepen your friendships with them and help them know personally the good news of Jesus Christ?

_____

_____

_____

CHAPTER SIX

Chair 2: The Believer

The person who moves from Chair 1 to Chair 2 has made an extraordinary transformation. She has not simply added Jesus to her life. She has been "made alive with Christ" (Ephesians 2:5). This is a total transformation of passing from the darkness to light, from death to life, from the kingdom of this world to the Kingdom of God. Christ's righteousness has been imputed to the new believer (Romans 5:17, 19). This is a radical inner transformation that needs to be celebrated. Baptism is the outward expression of this inner transformation, and should accompany this act of faith. For this reason baptism is one of a believer's first steps of obedience.

In other words, Chair 2 represents the new believer, the person who has just crossed the line, repented of his sin, put his faith in Christ and is now a "new creation in Christ." The old is gone and the new has come (2 Corinthians 5:17).

Despite this radical inner transformation, the Scriptures are clear: new believers need nurture and care to continue successfully in their new life. The New Testament uses two words to describe new believers. Hebrews 5:13 calls them infants: "Anyone who lives on milk, being still an infant, is not acquainted with the teaching about righteousness." The word used here is the Greek word *nepios* which indicates someone immature and totally dependent upon others. The second word, translated "child," is the word *teknion*. It has a similar connotation, but is used more as a term of affection toward a young child, a term of endearment I might use as a grandparent in reference to my wonderful grandkids. John uses the term often in his first epistle (1 John 2:1, 12, 28; 3:7, 18; 4:4; and 5:21). Both terms refer to a young believer, someone growing in the faith and learning the Christian life. They are dependent upon others for help and sustenance, need nurture and care. They need basic training and help developing basic skills.

My wife and I have the privilege of having five new grandchildren within the last three years. What an unspeakable joy! I've always loved children, but there is something special about loving your own grandchildren and watching them grow and mature. I was nervous at the birth of my own three daughters. Each time I worried if I'd be a good dad, raise them properly, and do all the right things. But with grandchildren, those fears are nonexistent. All I feel is pure love and joy. We enjoy watching them learn to walk, talk, and feed themselves. We celebrate little things, such as first steps and potty training. The joy is in the journey itself, the process of helping them grow.

And so should it be with spiritual children. The joy is in the journey. It is normal and natural to grow, make mistakes, and learn from them. It is normal and natural to start out dependent on others and then to learn to feed yourself, to learn to walk and talk, to learn to care for yourself. That means that, just as literal children needs parents, spiritual children need spiritual parents to lead them through this process.

THE PROCESS MODELED

Jesus understood this process. Early on in His ministry, when Jesus challenged the disciples to "follow me," He took His disciples to a wedding party up in Galilee and performed His first miracle (John 2:1–11). Making the journey to Galilee, attending the wedding, and then traveling to Capernaum for a "few days" with Jesus's mother and brothers meant that Jesus and His disciples were together for several days (John 2:12). No doubt this was a time of teaching, relationship building, answering basic questions, and deepening friendship. From there Jesus went up to the Passover and met with Nicodemus (John 2–3). "After this," John tells us in summary, "Jesus and his disciples (followers) went out into the Judean countryside, where he was spent some time with them, and baptized" (John 3:22).

Jesus took the time to get to know His followers, and they got to know Him. Relationships take time and growth takes time. Jesus knew there was no effective way to speed up this process. Jesus spent up to eighteen months just developing His disciples through this first stage.[1]

For Jesus and the initial followers, this was a critical stage of development. He was modeling life to them, modeling what it meant to walk as He walked, which He later commanded them to do (1 John 2:6). Jesus knew that in this first phase of life, much like in the early phases of child rearing, more is caught than taught. Children learn more by watching and participating than by taking notes. So He invested relationally in His young followers.

In these early months, Jesus modeled six foundational priorities for His new followers.[2] First, Jesus modeled full dependence upon the Holy Spirit. The Scriptures are clear—every aspect of Jesus's life and ministry was saturated with the Spirit of God. Jesus was conceived by the Spirit (Luke 1:35), anointed by the Spirit (Luke 4:18; Acts 10:38; Isaiah 61:1), filled with the Spirit (Luke 4:1, 14; John 3:34), sealed by the Spirit (John 6:27), led by the Spirit (Luke 4:1), rejoiced in the Spirit (Luke 10:21), gave commands by the Spirit (Acts 1:2), performed miracles by the power of the Spirit (Matthew 12:28; Luke 4:14–15, 18), was resurrected by the Spirit (Hebrews 9:14; Romans 8:11), and through the Spirit presented Himself fully obedient (Hebrews 9:14).

Second, Jesus modeled the centrality of prayer in His life and ministry. His ministry began in prayer (Luke 3:21) and ended in prayer (Luke 23:46). Shortly after His baptism the Spirit led Jesus into the wilderness (Luke 4:1), where He launched His ministry with forty days of fasting and prayer. The busier Jesus became, the more He slipped away to pray (Mark 6:31). Before every major decision Jesus makes, you find Him coming out of prayer (Luke 6:12). Over forty-five passages in the Gospels record how Jesus often slipped away to pray (Luke 5:16).

Third, Jesus modeled the importance of obedience to His Father's will. Early in Jesus's life, when He was twelve years old, Jesus was obedient to His earthly parents, Mary and Joseph (Luke 2:51). For His entire life He was obedient to His Heavenly Father. Obedience wasn't easy. He suffered for His obedience, and He learned obedience through what He suffered (Hebrews 2:18; 5:8). Jesus Himself said, "I seek not to please myself but him who sent me" (John 5:30) and that His will was to do what the Father desired, "Yet not my will but yours be done" (Luke 22:42). Later Jesus turned to His disciples and told them to "go and make disciples, teaching them *to obey* everything *I* have commanded you" (Matthew 28:19–20, italics added). Jesus knew that obedience was His Father's love language.

Fourth, God's Word was central in Christ's life and ministry. He modeled its use in every situation. Jesus knew the Word and used it as He encountered the everyday issues of life. He referred to the Old Testament more than eighty times, quoting from over seventy different chapters. Scripture was on His lips during His entire ministry, from the hour of His temptation to the moment of His death. Jesus wanted His disciples to know that He had not come to set aside the Scriptures but to fulfill them (Matthew 5:17). The Pharisees grieved Jesus because they didn't study the Word diligently. Jesus often said, "Have you never read what David did?" (Luke 6:3) or "Have you never read in the Law?" He rebuked the Sadducees for not studying the Word: "Are you not in error because you do not know the Scriptures?" (Mark 12:24). Jesus recognized Scripture as His guide for knowing the Father's will and understanding His own role in the world (John 13:1; 19:28).

Fifth, Christ consistently modeled the pattern of exalting His Father in every area of life. This was evident early in his ministry, as Jesus stated: "But whoever lives by the truth comes into the light, so that it may be seen plainly that what they have done has been done in the sight of God" (John 3:21). Toward the end of His ministry, Jesus still acknowledged that everything He had came from the Father: "Now they know that everything you have given me comes from you" (John 17:7). Again and again, Jesus claimed, "I do nothing on my own . . . rather, it is the Father, living in me, who is doing his work" (John 8:28; 14:10). Every part of Jesus's life exalted the Father and His union with His Father. In the same way, we are to exalt the Father in all that we do, following the example set for us by Jesus.

Sixth, Jesus modeled intentional relationships of love and integrity throughout His life. The very essence of the incarnation underscores this truth. "The Word became flesh and made his dwelling among us" (John 1:14). Early in His ministry, Jesus prioritized building relationships with a broad base of people. From these relationships Jesus later identified a few with whom He went deeper. But not only was Jesus proactive with the lost, but He intentionally pursued the initial disciples. Love was the basis of Jesus's relational life and He challenged the disciples to have the same love in their relationships. "As I have loved you," He commanded, "so you must love one another. By this all men will know that you are my disciples, if you love one another" (John 13:34–35).

These six priorities were foundational to the way Jesus lived His earthly life. When Jesus told His disciples to walk as He had walked, it was these priorities He wanted them to embody (1 John 2:6). It is these values new believers must see modeled by more mature believers as they start their Christian journey.

THE NEEDS OF NEW BELIEVERS

Helping children grow is not rocket science. As my wife and I enjoy our grandchildren, it is obvious what their immediate needs are. They need to know first and foremost who they belong to. Who is their family and who are their parents? In time, they need to learn how to walk and talk and feed themselves. They also need to learn, in time, how to clean themselves, or become potty trained.

It was critical to Jesus that He understand whom He belonged to. At His baptism, for the very first time, Jesus heard His Father's voice say, "This is my Son, whom I love; with him I am well pleased" (Matthew 3:17). In the Old Testament, learned rabbis would string together key verses from three major parts of the Old Testament to convey a truth. This was called stringing pearls.[3] At Jesus's baptism, God the Father did the same thing. He took references from three major portions of the Old Testament and strung them together to make a profound statement: "You are my son" (Psalm 2:7), "whom I love" (Genesis 22:2), "with you I am well pleased" (Isaiah 42:1). With these three brief citations, God spoke of Jesus as a king, a servant, and His son.

New believers also need to know their true identity, especially since that identity has been so radically altered at conversion. The Bible lists thirty-three things that happen the moment we come to Christ. We are chosen, adopted, forgiven, redeemed, included in Christ, sealed with the Holy Spirit, made alive, and seated with Him in the heavenly realm—and more![4] All of these transformations speak to our identity as followers of Christ. Our identity is essential to being able to know not only who we are but also *whose* we are. To move into Chair 3 as a worker, we must know whose we are, as this will be tested again and again, just as Satan tested Jesus right after His baptism. Understanding our identity in Christ is a lifelong journey, but we must begin immediately helping new believers understand their new identity. We can live victoriously for Christ when we understand who we are in Christ. We don't strive for victory; we live from victory. The battle has been won and we are on the winning team.

Second, new believers need to learn to walk on their own. My wife and I had the great privilege of having our oldest daughter and our two grandchildren living with us for six months, as our son-in-law finished seminary studies. During this time, our first grandson learned to crawl and then to walk and then started running. What a joy!

For hours we watched together with excitement as little Kellen began to crawl. Then we celebrated as he pulled himself to his feet up all by himself. He was such a proud little boy. He looked at all of us and grinned. Soon he began to push his walker and take some steps on his own. Then one day it happened. All on his own, he took off. He took his first steps. We all hurried into the room to watch him do it again and again, and we all cheered to his delight. Soon he was off to the races. And we have had a hard time keeping up with him ever since.

This delight, this joy we experienced—it should be no different as we watch new believers in Christ, spiritual children, begin to walk as Jesus walked. Trusting the Holy Spirit, saying their first prayer, obeying through difficulties, becoming Word-centered, exalting Jesus in everything, and then building new relationships with love and integrity. Children learn to walk because they see other people doing it—their parents and grandparents, maybe older siblings. But without models who demonstrate the way, this journey can take so much longer. Just as we helped our grandson learn to walk, so we must help new believers. Modeling the process, celebrating the little victories, and then helping them when they fall is not rocket science, but it does demand intentional effort.

New believers must also learn to talk. My wife and I wagered a bet. Which would our granddaughter, Keira, say first: "grandpa" or "grandma"? We spent so much time coaching her, each of us trying to teach her to say our own names. Boy was it fun! Progress was slow at first, but soon words began to come quicker and quicker. And sometimes not at the right times or in the right ways. But that's what makes the process so much fun.

One of my regrets when my children were growing up is that I failed to write down all the funny things they said. My oldest daughter Julie, when she was just four years old, came into the study where I was reading my Bible. She asked me what I was reading. Since I was in Hebrews 13:17–19, I told her that it said that we were to "obey our leaders, and not give them grief" (my translation for a three-year-old).

"Do you know what 'grief' means?" I asked.

She quickly answered, "Oh, I know!"

"What does it mean?" I asked.

"Well," she replied, "when Mommy makes me panny cakes (pancakes), she does that! She puts grief (grease) in the pan. So we aren't to give leaders any grief."

I still laugh about that exchange of words. Teaching children to talk can be as funny as it is challenging.

In the same way, new believers have to learn to speak—to tell God's Story and their own story. At the church I previously attended, just prior to baptism, new believers were required to write out their testimony. They were guided in writing out an account of their life before they came to Christ, how they came to Christ, and then describing their life since they trusted Christ. Each person was guided to tell their own story in a creative way, both in a thirty-second format and a longer format. Learning to tell their story, to give their testimony, helped them clarify in their own mind what God had done for them.

New believers also need to be able to understand and to tell God's story. When they are able to do so, they will be able to share how God's Story intersects with their personal story. This gives new meaning to their life and clarity to God's agenda. While this is a lifelong journey of knowing more and more about God's Story (the Bible), it is critical to know the basic elements of that Story from the beginning of their journey.

Each summer our North American ministry, Sonlife Ministries, brings several hundred students together at an event we call SEMP (Students Equipped to Minister to Peers). We spend several hours each morning teaching students how to summarize both God's Story and their personal story. We use a simple four-part outline: Creation, Fall, Rescue, and Restoration. After the training, students are sent out on the streets of Chicago to ask people about their story, to share God's Story, and then weave their personal story of redemption into God's Story. By the end of the week, students gain confidence and are instructed in how to write letters back home to their friends sharing that story and asking for a time to discuss it more. Every year we see many people come to faith, simply because these students share their stories.

New believers must eventually learn to feed themselves. Can you picture the mess—the mess a one-year-old boy makes when he insists upon feeding himself? I can, because I've lived it! Food on the floor. Food smeared all over the plate. Food in the hair. Occasionally some makes it in the mouth.

Maturity is a journey. We all began by making some messes as we tried to feed ourselves. We all insisted upon feeding ourselves, because we watched more mature adults doing it, so we wanted to do the same. In the same way, new spiritual children need to learn to feed themselves. They need to learn to open a Bible, dig into God's Word, and learn truth for themselves. They need to learn the importance of placing themselves under godly teachers who can feed them the meat of the Word and help them to dig it out for themselves.

Just as none of us like to see an older adult unable to feed themselves, so we don't want to see our children become the same way. Starting with milk, they need to graduate to the meat of God's Word. They need to learn good nutrition, taking in what is healthy and not trying to feed their spiritual life on empty calories or junk food. Simple study tools, such as inductive study—What does it say? What does it mean? How do I apply it to my life?—are a good beginning point. Knowing how to use concordances, Gospel harmonies, and online Bible study resources are helpful. Without some guidance, new believers will never mature to the meat of God's Word.

Finally, new believers must be potty trained. Our granddaughter, Elyse, visited us for a couple of weeks when she was in the process of learning to use the bathroom. When she had a successful trip to the potty, we all ran into the bathroom and clapped, just as we did with our own children. Elyse was so proud of herself. The whole family was celebrating the new lesson she'd learned. No more diapers! *Everyone* was excited!

One morning, I was awake early reading my Bible on our deck. Elyse came down the stairs to join Grandpa in his daily Bible reading. Still remembering her bathroom from the day before, Elyse let our golden retriever, Lucy, out the back door. She watched Lucy go out to the lawn and go to the bathroom. Elyse asked me what Lucy was doing. I told her, "She's doing what you did yesterday. She's going to the bathroom."

Immediately Elyse ran to the edge of our deck and began to clap for Lucy. "Grandpa," she said, "come and clap for Lucy." I laughed, but I went over to the deck's edge, and we clapped for Lucy!

Spiritual potty training is a simple lesson to learn. When we sin, we need to deal with the sin and get back in the power of God's Spirit. We need to learn how to live a cleansed life. I will discuss this more in the next chapter, but new Christians need to learn the basic skills of confessing sin, claiming God's forgiveness, and then walking in the power of the Holy Spirit. Perhaps one of the most helpful tools here is the simple, "How to Experience God's Love and Forgiveness" booklet by Campus Crusade. Early in my Christian life, I was trained by CRU staff on how to spiritually breathe—to exhale (confess the sin) and then inhale (claim God's forgiveness). This simple little tool saved many wasted hours of trying to live in the power of the flesh and freed me to live in the power of God's Spirit.

PRINCIPLES FOR MINISTRY TO PEOPLE IN CHAIR 2

When working with Chair 2 people, keep these four principles in mind:

1) First, without immediate nurture, new Christians will struggle and, in many cases, they won't survive. An infant needs the embrace of physical parents. They are totally dependent upon what the parents provide or don't provide. New Christians are no different. New Christians must become a priority. We cannot just assume they can care for themselves. Just as we prioritize a new baby in the home, so we must prioritize time with new spiritual children.

2) Second, we must give personalized attention to the basics of the Christian life. Simple lessons such as learning our identity, learning how to walk, talk, feed ourselves, and clean ourselves need to be celebrated. We can't assume new believers will know how to do these things themselves. We have a lifetime to master these basics, but immediate and simple help can be taught early to ensure success. Moreover, as we invest in new believers, we model for them how to care for their new believers as they grow. We tend to duplicate with others how we have been treated. Good nurture of new believers ensures future success with the next generation.

3) Third, we must not forget the importance of our identity in Christ. Without knowing Whose we are, we become susceptible to a wide array of false teachings. A secure identity goes a long way in producing confidence in our walk with God.

4) Spiritual children need a family. It is in a family that values are learned, lessons are taught, and love is experienced. The church family needs to be that family for new spiritual babies. We will discuss this more in later chapters, but nothing is more joyful than to have parents, grandparents, older brothers and sisters, around the same table. The four chairs we're discussing need to be circled to complete the picture of what God wants His bride to be like. It is when all the ages come together, that we experience the complete joy of being the family of God.

Moving from Chair 1 to Chair 2 is an unparalleled transformation from darkness to light, life to death. As important as that move is, it's just the beginning. It is important that we work intentionally with new believers to help them move from Chair 2 to Chair 3.

PONDERINGS

1. What do you remember about how you were treated as a new believer? Was it a good or poor experience?

_____

_____

2. What do you believe is the most important first step for new Christians? Explain your answer.

_____

_____

3. Take a few minutes to identify a couple of new believers you can help grow in the basics discussed in this chapter.

_____

_____

_____

CHAPTER SEVEN

Chair 3: The Worker

Eighteen months into His ministry, Jesus made a radical move. He issued His third challenge to a group of four men—James and John, Simon and Andrew. "Follow me," He said, "and I will make you fishers of men" (Matthew 4:19; Mark 1:17 ESV). Jesus singled out these two sets of brothers for a deepened investment. They were not yet the Twelve, although they all became a part of His Twelve eventually. At this point, they were in Chair 3.

Perhaps the best term to describe someone in Chair 3 is a "worker" or "young man." He is a teenager of sorts, someone who is no longer a child, but not yet a parent. Young men are zealous for action and becoming independent. They have mastered some basic skills and desire to be others-oriented. Whereas a child or infant (Chair 2) is "me" oriented—in a healthy way—a Chair 3 person begins putting others before their own interests. They become aware of the needs of others and begin to experience the joys of serving others and being productive.

Workers are engaged in the work of ministry. While working within the Body of Christ (the church), they are also laboring in the field (the world). They are concerned about bringing in the harvest. I call this peer care (within the body) and peer share (within the harvest field). Peer care is caring for younger believers, and peer share is caring for unbelievers.

We may be tempted to think of a worker as someone busy within the church, but Jesus had a different perspective of the need for workers. He was moved with compassion as He looked upon the crowds. They were "harassed and helpless, like sheep without a shepherd" (Matthew 9:36). So Jesus took action. He called His disciples to be part of the solution. "The harvest is plentiful," He said, "but the workers are few. Ask the Lord of the harvest, therefore, to send out workers into his harvest field" (Matthew 9:37–38). The Father was the Lord of the harvest. What He lacked were workers to send into the field. So Jesus did the very thing He told His disciples to pray for: He sent out His disciples two by two into the harvest field, equipping them to share their faith with authority, becoming true "fishers of men" (Matthew 10:1–4).

A worker is not yet fully trained, but he is moving in that direction (Luke 6:40). He is stepping out in faith and experiencing God working through him. In Luke 10, the disciples are full of joy as they experienced God using them. Jesus is also "full of joy by the Holy Spirit," because He was seeing the fruit of His laser focus upon "making disciples who could make disciples." They were growing in maturity and gaining experience. It was important that they be prepared, because Jesus soon would commission them to "go and bear fruit," even to "all nations" (John 15:16; Matthew 28:19).

Having worked as a youth pastor for years and raised my own three daughters through their teen years, I have learned to love this stage of life. Energy, zeal, unbridled passion, and invincibility are all characteristics of this stage. Teens are willing to step out and try new things. They have a teachable spirit, which makes this stage of life full of new experiences. They long to be given the chance both to fail and to succeed. If they fail, we need to be there to help pick them up. If they succeed, we need to be there to remind them of the source of their success.

Regardless, energy tends to rule the day. "I'll try anything once," is a common motto among young workers.

Working with teenagers can be both joyful and demanding, all on the same day. Sometimes they act like adults and they amaze us with their keen insight and fresh views. Then, at a moment's notice, they can revert to childishness and become angry, discouraged, or self-centered. It is all a part of the growing-up process. Developing workers can have the same ups and downs. That's why we find Jesus seventeen times spending time with the masses but forty-six times with these few followers.[1] If they were going to mature, He needed to invest in them.

Jesus offers a clear picture of what a maturing worker looks like. While not fully trained or completely mature, they are moving in that direction. They are in search of more. In Luke 4:42–44, Jesus had just returned with His disciples from a "missions" trip, preaching in the synagogues of Galilee with His disciples (Luke 4:42–44).[2] The trip could have taken as long as two months, because they visited all the synagogues in Galilee. However long the trip was exactly, it's clear Jesus's disciples were away from their fishing business for a period of time.

Upon returning, I'm sure they felt the pressure of paying the bills and meeting the needs of everyday life. I'm sure Peter's wife (I like to call her Ruthie) liked that her husband spent time with Jesus, who had healed her mother. Even so, I'm sure she was still very concerned about meeting the family's daily needs. So after a long missions trip with Jesus, Peter and his buddies returned to their fishing business to earn a living, only to spend the night catching nothing (Luke 5:5). I'm sure they were not in a good mood. Ruthie was not going to be happy. They had been serving with Jesus, and now this is what they get? A crowd had gathered on the northern shore of the Sea of Galilee to buy fish from the night's catch. This time there was nothing to buy. Jesus comes walking by the marketplace, and the crowds immediately begin to gather around Him (Luke 5:1).

You get the impression that the disciples are off to the side, not involved with the teaching. Perhaps they are still steaming, because they've just spent a night of hard work with no fish to show for it. Jesus climbs in Peter's boat and pushes out from the shore. Peter is probably washing the nets with the other disciples, wrapping up the disappointing night's work. Jesus tells Peter to "put out into the deep water, and let down the nets for a catch." Peter responds begrudgingly, "We have worked hard all night and haven't caught a thing. But because you say so, I will let down the nets."

From this text we can glean several insights into the characteristics of Chair 3 people. First and foremost, the disciples were available (Luke 5:1–3). They were present and allowed Jesus to use their boat. When Jesus called them into service, they were willing to respond.

Second, they were faithful as they responded to Jesus's difficult request. He told them to put their nets down out in the deep for a catch (5:4–5). They had fished all night and had caught nothing—the morning hours were not the time to try again. And definitely not out in the deep, as it was in the shallow of the spring waters of the northern shores where fish gathered. But they obeyed, faithfully doing as Jesus requested.

Third, they were teachable (5:6–8), willing to do what the Master requested, even though they had worked hard all night and caught nothing. Against all practical wisdom, they were willing to learn any new lessons that only obedience could bring them.

Fourth, they were enthusiastic about the new lessons they were learning. When they saw what Jesus did, Peter was quick to call in his partners. I can imagine the excitement as both boats almost sank due to the large catch of fish. "When Peter saw this," he dropped to his knees and exclaimed, "Go away from me, Lord; I am a sinful man" (5:7–8).

And finally, they were responsive to Jesus and His leadership, as they responded again to His repeated challenge to come and "catch men." They were not perfect, but they were seeking AFTER more— available, faithful, teachable, enthused about the things of God, and responsive to leadership. These are all qualities to look for in faithful workers.

THE PROCESS MODELED

Making the decision to prioritize a few disciples was a defining moment in the life of Christ. I would call it one of the major defining moments of Christ's entire ministry strategy. Having just faced rejection in His hometown of Nazareth (Luke 4:28–29), Jesus is now faced with a number of new events.[3] Jesus leads His ministry through four major transitional issues during this time.

First was a transition of leadership. In Matthew 4:12–22, Jesus receives news that His cousin John has been put in prison. How alarming it must have been for Jesus and His family knowing that Herod Antipas had been watching the Jesus movement grow and placing his spies in the crowds to report what was happening. John was the leader of this movement and multitudes were coming out to hear him speak and to be baptized. John was like the Billy Graham of His day, eventually amassing disciples over 300 miles away.[4] John was providing cover for Jesus, allowing Him time to build His own team and spend time with His disciples. John knew that eventually, "He must become greater; I must become less" (John 3:30). John's imprisonment had to have been difficult for Jesus and His family. John's execution later would have an even greater impact on Jesus as He sought to get away to a solitary place when He received news of John's death (Matthew 14:13; Mark 6:30-31). Jesus, in John's absence, became leader of this movement.

Second, Jesus experienced a transition of location. Realizing the political tensions and regional transitions happening, Jesus decided to relocate His ministry eighteen miles to the east in Capernaum (Matthew 4:13–16). He had been working in Nazareth, a small community of twenty or thirty families tucked away from the major transportation routes. Possibly consisting of a group of families of the lineage of David, they were probably isolating themselves from others to await the coming of the Messiah.[5]

Even though the Messiah had appeared in their midst, they continued to reject Him, saying in Matthew 13:54–56, "'Where did this man get this wisdom and these miraculous powers? Isn't this the carpenter's son? Isn't his mother's name Mary, and aren't his brothers James, Joseph, Simon and Judas? Aren't all his sisters with us? Where then did this man get all these things?' And they took offense at him."

From this remote place, Jesus went to Capernaum, a larger and more strategic city in the region. Located on the Via Maris or "The Way of the Sea" highway, it was the major trade route connecting Egypt with the northern empires of Mesopotamia. Capernaum was large enough to host a centurion with his soldiers, a royal official and his family, and several tax collectors. It was the crossroads of the region, and anyone traveling through the area traveled through Capernaum. Located on the beautiful shoreline of the Sea of Galilee, it was a prosperous town with a large Jewish contingency and a major synagogue for the area. Many have called this region the evangelical triangle. It was in the small region of Capernaum, Bethsaida, and Korazin that Jesus performed most of His miracles, a region of just a few square miles and easily traveled by foot.

Third, Jesus experienced a transition of message. The text tells us that, at this point, Jesus picked up the message of John the Baptist. "From that time on," we read, "Jesus began to preach, 'Repent, for the kingdom of heaven has come near'" (Matthew 4:17). This statement makes me wonder, What was Jesus preaching before this point? Was He preaching at all, or just investing in His few disciples?

During the initial eighteen months of Jesus's ministry, which began with His baptism, Jesus called people to Himself, explaining to them that He was the Messiah, and spending time with them. But now Jesus inherits a movement of baptized followers, a movement that was gaining steam. And His message was clear: repent. He was calling them not to turn over a new leaf but to find a new life. Entrance into the Kingdom begins with repentance, turning from the way of sin and turning to the source of life. His message also announced the Kingdom of God. More than eighty times Jesus references this Kingdom. At least seven times He says that the Kingdom is "near" or had "come upon them" (Matthew 4:17; 10:7; Mark 1:15; 12:34; Luke 10:9, 11; 21:31). He tells the "secrets" of the Kingdom (Mark 4:11) and gives eight examples of what the Kingdom is "like" (Matthew 13:24, 31, 44, 45, 47; 18:23; 22:2; Mark 4:26, 30). In the book of Acts, after His resurrection and during the forty days He appeared to His disciples, He "spoke to them about the Kingdom of God" (Acts 1:3).

The apostles and disciples continued to preach the Good News of the Kingdom of God and the name of Jesus (Acts 8:12; 19:8; 28:23). The very last verse of the book of Acts describes Paul boldly preaching, "the Kingdom of God and teaching about the Lord Jesus Christ" (Acts 28:31). As a result of this message, over eighteen times the Gospels record that the "news spread everywhere." This was a bold message filled with expectation and hope.

Fourth, Jesus experienced a transition of calling. Jesus now steps up the challenge. He calls four disciples, with whom He has just spent the last several months, into Chair 3, to become workers in the harvest field. Gone were the days of just "come and see" or "follow me." Now there is a new challenge. *Become part of My team, My ministry team, Jesus charged, and I will teach you how to reproduce. Ultimately you will lead your own family of disciple-makers under My authority and through My power.*

The disciples did not realize fully at this point that this challenge would involve servanthood, sacrifice, and suffering. It would demand more than they could ever realize and offer more than they could ever comprehend—for now and eternity. It would require them to understand their own limits, recognizing that in and of themselves they could never accomplish this challenge. They would have to learn full dependence upon the Holy Spirit power, learn to walk as Jesus walked, no matter what they faced. It was the beginning of a radically new lifestyle. It truly was a new adventure and would ultimately lead to the final challenge (Chair 4) of "go and bear fruit" (John 15:16). From this point on, the disciples become the priority of Jesus. They were His future. Their success at learning to become "fishers of men" would determine the future of the Christian movement.

THE NEEDS OF WORKERS

When disciples make the transition from spiritual childhood to their spiritual teens, their needs of growth and development change radically. Perhaps one of the greatest needs believers have at this stage is to see and experience God using them.

When I was a new Christian, I was sent to O'Hare International Airport in Chicago to share my faith for the first time. Scared and excited, I circled a stranger several times trying to work up the courage to ask him a few questions. This was a new challenge for me—intentionally approaching someone and initiating a spiritual conversation. After about thirty minutes of convincing myself that I could do this, I approached a man sitting at the American Airlines baggage claim.

I'll never forget that conversation. I was a brand-new Christian, and he was working on his PhD in philosophy of religion at the University of Chicago. He chewed me up and spit me out. I couldn't understand half of his questions or half of his words. All I could say was, "Once I was blind, but now I see." It didn't go well. I wanted to quit. *This is not for me*, I thought. *I am not an evangelist.*

But I decided to try once more. I went upstairs at O'Hare and found another person to practice on. He had just stepped off a plane and was sitting down. I waited a moment, hoping he'd get up and leave. He didn't. Finally, summoning every last ounce of courage I had, I approached him with a couple of questions from a spiritual survey. He was open and eager to talk. I didn't know how to handle this.

I pulled out an evangelism booklet and asked if I could share it with him. He said, "Yes, I'd love for you to." Then he pulled the same booklet out of his shirt pocket. He had just come from Philadelphia where another student had shared the same booklet with him, but he only read half of it before he boarded the plane. He had been thinking about it the whole trip. As I had been trained, I began reading the whole booklet from the beginning. He was always one step ahead of me. He finally asked me straight out, "What must I do to know Christ personally?" With tears in his eyes, he prayed and asked Christ to come into his life. He thanked me for talking with him. For months we corresponded about his newfound faith and his personal growth. I would never be the same again! I experienced God working through me, and the experience changed me forever.

Chair 3 people (workers) need this experience. It may mean something as simple as caring for a baby in a nursery and experiencing God's pleasure. It may mean having the opportunity to share your story or ministering to a senior citizen by teaching God's Word. The experience is not just religious activity. It is something that instills the sense that God is using me. He is working through me. I am seeing the spiritual happen, lives are being touched and I know it's not me. It is God. This is the reason I was created, to be a vessel through whom God could flow. I want more!

One of the most critical lessons to be learned in Chair 3 is the "new way" of living in the Spirit. Ministering in the Spirit. Loving in the

Spirit. Serving in the Spirit. Giving in the Spirit. Dying to self through the Spirit. Victory over sin by the Spirit.

I've seen it happen so many times. People come to Christ, they begin to grow, and they want to be used by God. They volunteer as a Sunday school teacher, a worker in the nursery, an usher, or a counselor after an outreach event. They try to reach out to their neighbors or work associates because they've heard this is what they should be doing. In the fear of the moment, the busyness of life, the challenge of a new project, they decide to work really hard at this spiritual endeavor. They give it their best. After several weeks or several months, they find themselves worn out, tired, disillusioned. It didn't go the way they were hoping. Problems surfaced, conflicts arose, frustration came from within. The joy is gone. What went wrong?

Paul describes a similar situation in Romans 7. "I know that good itself does not dwell in me, that is, in my sinful nature. For I have the desire to do what is good, but I cannot carry it out. For I do not do the good I want to do, but the evil I do not want to do—this I keep on doing."

He then goes on, "what a wretched man I am! Who will rescue me from this body that is subject to death?" (Romans 7:24). Twenty-nine times in Romans 7 Paul says "I . . . I . . . I." But in the very next chapter, Paul gives the glorious answer to his conundrum. It is the Spirit who gives us the victory. Nineteen times in Romans 8, Paul explains it is "the Spirit" who will live within us, set us free, and help us serve in "the new way of the Spirit" (Romans 7:6).

The Spirit-filled life is the victory that sets us free. It is the *new way*; it is the only way. There are many ways to describe this lifestyle: the exchanged life, the Spirit-filled life, the crucified life. Without learning this new way of living, a Chair 3 person will be doomed to frustration, legalism, burnout, a loss of joy, an unproductive lifestyle. But most of all, they will be unable to get to Chair 4. The only way to Chair 4 is through Chair 3. And the lessons of Chair 3 must be learned. Romans 8 living is essential in this journey.

Moving into Chair 3 in our Christian journey demands learning new skills. Skills such as learning to run with endurance—not just walk. Learning to feed yourself and others—not just depending upon someone to feed you. Learning to defend God's Story and in a deeper way tell your story. Learning to deal with deep-seated sin and pursue holiness on a deeper level. All of these are skills needed to move to maturity. And this list is obviously not exhaustive.

Ephesians 4:12 speaks to the role of leaders within the Body of Christ. They are to "equip the saints for the work of service" (NASB). The word translated "equip" is the Greek word *katartizo*, which has a double meaning: to repair and to prepare. When Jesus called James and John to follow Him in Matthew 4:21, it says they were preparing (*katartizo*) their nets. Fishermen in the first century, at the end of a long day of fishing, had to *repair* any broken sections of their nets in order to *prepare* them for the next day's usage.

In the same way, as we move into Chair 3 and begin to be engaged more aggressively in the battles of life and ministry, we will soon recognize ways in which we are broken vessels and need to be *repaired*. Time in the battle tends to reveal these wounds. At the same time, as we begin to help others grow, we need to be *prepared* to share the Good News with Chair 1 people, and then what it means to change diapers, feed babies, and nurture new Christ-followers in Chair 2. We need to be prepared to help others learn these basic skills in order to succeed. All of these are skills needed to eventually move toward the birthing of our own family in Chair 4.

Chair 3 disciples must also learn endurance. Back when I ran cross-country in school, my coach would always say, "Set a good pace that you can maintain long term; you'll end up much farther if you do." Too often inexperienced runners start the long distance race at a pace that neither they nor others can keep. Well short of the finish line, they collapse unable to finish. The runners who run the farthest are ultimately those who pace themselves well. In the zeal of ministry excitement, new workers need to learn to pace themselves well.

But even more than good pacing, we see in Jesus's life another powerful picture. Right after Jesus explains to His disciples that He must go to Jerusalem and suffer many things at the hands of the elders, chief priests, and teachers of the Law—including being killed (Matthew 16)—He then goes on a six-day journey with three of His disciples up to the Mount of Transfiguration. Luke 9:31 tells us that, there with Moses and Elijah, "they spoke about his departure, which he was about to bring to fulfillment at Jerusalem."

Could it be, that even Jesus, in His humanity needed encouragement about what He was about to face? Could it be that the heavenly Father, who spoke for the second time with a voice from heaven, "This is my Son, whom I have chosen, listen to Him," knew that His Son needed to hear from Him, and even from Moses and Elijah, about what was coming? I don't know for sure. But from this point on, over the next nine months as Jesus sets His face toward the suffering and sacrifice coming, you find Him at least ten times speaking about returning to His heavenly home.

His focus now becomes what was beyond the finish line! We are told in Hebrews 12:2 that Jesus, "who for the joy set before him he endured the cross, scorning its shame." Could it be that we too, will never make it through the suffering and sacrifice required in Chair 3, if we don't keep our eyes focused on what is beyond the cross that we all need to bear? A good runner looks beyond the finish line. Jesus clearly focused on the "joy set before him and endured the cross." In that same passage, Jesus, after telling His disciples that He must go to Jerusalem and die, then tells His disciples that they too, "must deny themselves and take up their cross and follow me" (Matthew 16:24).

PRINCIPLES FOR MINISTRY TO PEOPLE IN CHAIR 3

There are several very practical principles that we can identify in Chair 3 living.

1) Chair three is not easy, but it is our joy. Paul says it this way: "I want to know Christ—yes, to know the power of his resurrection and participation in his sufferings, becoming like him in his death" (Philippians 3:10). What does it mean to "become like him in his death?" As I reflect on the nine months leading up to Jesus's announcement that He must go to Jerusalem to die, I can identify some very clear truths about what it means to "become like him in his death."

First we know that it means being willing. In John 10:18 Jesus clearly states, "No one takes it [my life] from me, but I lay it down of my own accord. I have authority to lay it down and authority to take it up again. This command I received from my Father."

Second, we know it means dying intentionally. "As the time approached for him to be taken up to heaven, Jesus resolutely set out for Jerusalem," Luke 9:51 tells us. Jesus was not a victim. He committed to His mission and saw it through to the end.

Third, we know it means dying graciously and lovingly. Jesus never retaliated when He was insulted, never made threats when He suffered, never cried out along the painful journey (Isaiah 42:2, I Peter 2:21–22).

Fourth, we know it means He courageously faced His cross. So many times He could have escaped. Even the very last evening before His betrayal. But He courageously faced His cross and, living out the words of Psalm 44:22: "Yet for your sake we face death all day long; we are considered as sheep to be slaughtered."

Fifth, we find Jesus enduring the opposition against Him. He was mocked, ridiculed, spat upon, and beaten. All the weight of the brutal Roman crucifixion was imposed upon Him. Yet He deserved none of it. Hebrews 12:2 says He "endured" this cross. In the next few verses, we are told to "Consider him who endured such opposition from sinners, so that you will not grow weary and lose heart" (12:3).

Finally, we see Jesus, during this journey to His death, "entrusting himself to him who judges justly" (1 Peter 2:23). "Into your hands I commit my spirit" were His last words (Luke 23:46).

I believe Jesus was able to have this attitude as He willingly moved toward the cross, because His focus was not on the cross, but on the joy *beyond* the cross. Who "for the joy set before him he endured the cross, scorning its shame" (Hebrews 12:2). Like a runner running a marathon, Jesus focused beyond the finish line. His focus was on the joy set before Him. In the same way, we can learn to "deny ourselves and take up our cross daily," as we learn to focus beyond the finish line for the joy set before us!

Chair 3 means learning the lifelong lessons of "becoming like him in his death." This is a willingness to, in the same way, pick up our cross daily, to intentionally set our hearts on this journey, to graciously and lovingly treat well those who mistreat us, to courageously face our privileged calling, to endure opposition, and finally to entrust ourselves to the One who judges justly. What a privilege! But what a challenge, becoming like Him in His death.

Following the example of Jesus in this way makes us part of a fellowship of participation in his sufferings" (Philippians 3:10).It is a fellowship that goes beyond anything this world can offer. It is an unspoken sweetness and aroma experienced by those who know Christ and seek to make Him known. It is the treasure that makes everything else pale in comparison, that makes every other gain seem like a loss (Philippians 3:8).

The only way to reach Chair 4, spiritual parenting, is through Chair 3. Chair 3 is hard, but all of us must go through it. It is a life of suffering, servanthood, and sacrifice. It is our calling. It is a great privilege. It is a life of joyful victory, overflowing with His grace during the difficulties of following Him. It is not easy, but it is right. It is not free of problems, but it is our joy and privilege. It is the journey through which the Lord in His wisdom has chosen to build in us the character and priorities of Christ, and it is the deep longing of all our hearts—to be like Him.

2) Many believers do not make it through Chair 3. I wish it were not true. But I must be honest. Many believers do not make it past Chair 3. In order to make it through the challenges of Chair 3, we must be aware of what is coming, and make a conscious choice to persevere.

Early in the Christian journey, when the time is right, I like to talk to new believers about what Jesus went through when He faced the cross. I try to help them imagine what Jesus was experiencing when He predicted His death in Matthew 16, what He was feeling, and what He was telling His disciples. Peter responded to Jesus's news that He was going to Jerusalem to suffer and die, by saying, "Never, Lord! This shall never happen to you" (Matthew 16:22). Jesus rebuked Peter and said, "Get behind me, Satan! You are a stumbling block to me; you do not have in mind the concerns of God, but merely human concerns" (16:23).

In His humanity, taking the easy route was a temptation for Jesus. But Jesus did what He was called to do. And then Jesus says to His disciples, in the same way, "If anyone would come after me, he must deny himself, take up his cross and follow me." And where was Jesus headed, toward Jerusalem, where He laid down His life for others, a life of suffering and servanthood and sacrifice. It costs to be a Christ-follower! But the reward beyond the cross is well worth the price, and like Jesus, we must keep that joy before us as we endure our cross.

3) It takes time to mature to parenthood. So many of us want the benefits of parenthood without the pain of getting there. So many of us want spiritual children, but not the life of hard work, disciplined living, sacrificial giving, and hours of prayer and concern. Maturity takes time. It can't be rushed. Teen years are fun, but most everyone who is finished with them says, "I'm glad that is done!"

To the mature, immaturity seems like such a necessity to get through. But to the maturing, it can feel like such a long journey. Be encouraged: time is a wonderful developer of maturity. Allow God to mold and shape you. Allow Him to work in your life, teaching you the tough lessons. Don't shrink back, but lean into difficulties with faith and endurance (Hebrews 10:38–39). And after you have endured, you will reap the reward of the harvest.

4) Relax and enjoy the journey. Very early in my Christian life, I longed to be like Jesus. I was eager to engage with Him in making disciples who could make disciples. I wanted so badly to see a movement of multiplying disciples happening. And I wanted it immediately!

The Lord sent me off to Bible school, and for three years I realized how little I knew about Him. I began to see increasingly that the greatest problem I was facing was me! I ended up going through a number of years of very painful experiences, always asking, "Why, God?" I found myself facing conflicts and having to learn to deal with them. I found myself being falsely accused and facing painful rejection. More times than not, my life wasn't going that well. People misunderstood my intentions.

But through all this, God had a master plan that He was working for me. I see that now. I needed to go on this journey and learn everything I could. Nothing came my way that He had not approved in advance. He was shaping my life and molding it, to further serve Him. When I learned this simple lesson, I began to relax and enjoy the journey. God was doing what only God could do. He was moving me into maturity, making me more into the image of His Son. I needed to relax, rejoice in Him and learn all the lessons He was teaching me, and then allow Him to do what only He could do.

Chair 3 is a critical time of development for growing believers. And that development is leading to Chair 4.

PONDERINGS

1. After reading this chapter, how do you feel about Chair 3? Be honest.

_____

_____

_____

2. What are some major lessons you have had to learn on your journey as a worker for Christ?

_____

_____

_____

_____

3. Read Hebrew 10:32–12:15. This passage is all about Chair 3 living. What lessons do you see in these verses?

_____

_____

_____

_____

CHAPTER EIGHT

Chair 4:
The Disciple-Maker

hair 4 describes the fully trained disciple-maker. Luke 6:40 tells us that, "The student is not above the teacher, but everyone who is fully trained will be like their teacher." The word translated "fully trained" is the Greek word *katartizo*, the same word that can be translated "equipped." Jesus's ministry agenda was to birth a movement of multiplying disciples. To make that happen, He needed fully equipped disciples who were capable of making disciples who could make other disciples. This was the laser focus of Jesus in all of His dealings with His disciples: equipping them to become "fishers of men" (Matthew 4:19) and then commanding them to "Go and make disciples of all nations" (Matthew 28:19).

Because we want to imitate this focus, Southeast Christian Church (where I currently attend) has defined our training mission as "making disciples who can make disciples." Even though Matthew 28 tells us to make disciples, we felt it critical to use the phrase "making disciples who can make disciples," because to most people, disciple-making is just another deeper Bible study. We feel it is important to define success in terms of reproduction.

In fact, we have tried to do away with the word "discipleship" altogether. The term "discipleship" was first used extensively in 1850 by a man named Charles Adams, who broke the phrase "making disciples" into two parts—bringing people to Christ, which he labeled "evangelism," and then growing people up in Christ, which he labeled "discipleship."[1] He wrote articles about the two different wings of the airplane: evangelism and discipleship. People began to debate which was the most important. Some denominations even built buildings devoted just to evangelism and others devoted just to discipleship and then fought over which should get the most funding.

I fly a lot, and when I'm 35,000 feet up in the air, I don't look out the window and wonder which wing is most important. I want them both! Without both wings you will never get off the ground, climb to great heights, and soar. You certainly won't land without both. And the same is true in making disciples. Both wings—evangelism and discipleship—are critical. Without evangelism you cannot develop fully trained disciples, nor will you have any new disciples. And without discipleship you will not have any equipped disciples to go out and share their faith.

By defining our mission as "making disciples who can make disciples," Southeast Christian Church is seeking to define the end product of our efforts as reproduction, which includes both "evangelism" and "discipleship." We measure success by multiplication.

When my first daughter was born, my wife and I began to ask questions we had never asked before. "How do I change a diaper?" "What do I feed my new baby?" "How do I teach her to walk and talk?" These are all basic questions, but we expressed them with new urgency and seriousness. We were parents now, and we needed to know! The questions didn't stop there. My wife and I continued to grow and learn as we faced the new challenges of parenting children at each stage of development. We had a real family and wanted to see that family grow, be healthy, and multiply.

Moving into Chair 4 means a person has become a spiritual parent. A disciple-maker understands the journey of discipleship and has experienced success along that journey. He no longer is just learning how to be a "fisher of men" but now has seen people come to Christ, has learned how to grow them into reproducing disciples, and is beginning to see a family of seekers, new believers, and growing workers formed under his mentorship. She has now become a parent who is witnessing multiplication. Soon, as the journey progresses, she will experience the joy of being a grandparent and even a great-grandparent. Each step on this path requires new skills and priorities.

Another interesting phrase used in the Bible to describe the Chair 4 person is found in John 15:15. Throughout his Gospel, John shows the progression of the disciples' growth and relationship to Jesus. They begin as seekers (John 1), then become followers (John 4), then coworkers or servants (John 13). Finally Jesus makes an amazing statement. "I no longer call you servants," He tells his disciples, "because a servant does not know his master's business. Instead, I have called you friends, for everything that I learned from my Father I have made known to you" (John 15:15). Wow! Like Moses and like Abraham before them, they are now identified as "friends of God" (Exodus 33:11; 2 Chronicles 20:7; James 2:23).

Friendship goes beyond servanthood. We long to meet with friends. We are free at any time to call our friends and pour out our heart to them. Friendship involves a deepened relationship, a freedom to enter into one another's presence, a security of position. As God's friends, we no longer strive to please Him because we realize we are accepted and beloved. We enter into a rest and joy in the Lord's presence. We know the relationship is not about us but about what He has done for us.

My wife and I through the years have had a great privilege of having many good friends. For over ten years we hosted a book club full of godly people. Through the years, deep friendships formed in that group. We have laughed so hard we have cried. At times, we have cried so hard that we had to back up and laugh. We are deep friends and now, even though we are separated by distance, we still meet together. When we do, we immediately pick up where we last left off. We are deep friends who enjoy being together. We know each other's strengths and weaknesses and still love each other!

In the same way, after years of walking with the Lord, I can testify to this stage of relationship with Him. No longer striving or trying hard to win God's favor, I've learned that I have His favor due to the Cross. I can be myself. I love to meet with the Lord. I long to be in His presence. I am assured of His love, because I know that He knows more about me than I know about me—and He loves me anyway! We are friends, and I marvel at that privilege. Jesus says that those disciples who reach Chair 4 are His friends. What an honor!

THE PROCESS MODELED

No one passage captures this reality for me better than Luke 10. Almost three and a half years into the ministry of Christ, Jesus is making His final approach into Jerusalem for His last Passover, where He will be betrayed and offered up on the Cross. About six months earlier (see Luke 9) Jesus sent His twelve Apostles out two by two to preach the Kingdom of God and to heal the sick. They came back full of joy.

But in Luke 10, Jesus sends out seventy-two disciples. These are the Chair 3 people, the next generation of workers. He sent them to go before Him into every town and place where He was about to go because, "The harvest is plentiful, but the workers are few" (Luke 10:2). After a short time of sharing the Good News, being engaged in fishing for men, they returned "with joy" (Luke 10:17), just as the Twelve had in Luke 9. Jesus Himself was also "full of joy through the Holy Spirit" (Luke 10:21). Three times in the Bible it is recorded that Jesus wept (John 11:35; Luke 19:41; Hebrews 5:7), but only here does it record that Jesus is "full of joy." What made Him so happy?

I'm convinced the reason is simple. At this moment, after three and a half years of pouring Himself into His disciples, He now knows they are at the point that they can invest in others. His efforts to build a movement of multiplying disciples are now bearing fruit. He knows that 2,000 years later, you and I will also be Christ-followers because His ministry calling was being realized. He had made disciples who would make disciples. Clearly His mission was not to reach the world, as much as it was to make disciples who could reach the world. He was about birthing a movement of multiplying disciples, and this was being realized before His very eyes.

Over four years, Jesus had taken His disciples from seekers (John 1:39) to followers (John 10:27) to coworkers (Matthew 4:19) and then finally to disciple-makers (Luke 10:2). Then He told them to do what He had done with them: to go and make disciples of all nations. Jesus modeled the process by which they must do that. The book of Acts shows the disciples following through with this command. Acts can be outlined according to the Commission given in Acts 1:8. The work began in Jerusalem in Acts 2:5, moved into Judea and Samaria in Acts 8:5, and continued throughout the remainder of the earth in Acts 8:26. The disciples went out and duplicated the process, making disciples who could make disciples.

On my computer is a list of 187 people that I have labeled "people I love." These are men and women I would do most anything for. They are men who are multiplying their lives into others, making disciples who can make disciples. I pray for them regularly and contact them as often as possible. I claim them as my disciples, even though many people contribute to making a fully trained disciple. Let me tell you just a few stories.

Mark was in my youth group. At the age of fifteen he committed his life to Christ and began to reach out to his friends. Later he worked with me when I led Sonlife Ministries. Now he lives in Costa Rica, making disciples who can make disciples. Mark's disciples in Latin America are now being sent around the world.

Annette is a good friend and a successful businesswoman. As she moved from being a seeker to a growing believer, God challenged Annette to participate in a mission trip to Haiti. Soon the Lord challenged Annette and her husband to move to Chair 4, to step out in faith and do something they had never done before. God spoke to Annette about building a hospital in Haiti. Annette faithfully raised the funds and began her own ministry, and now the hospital is flourishing and touching lives. People are being reached for Christ, are growing in the Lord, and being sent out to do the same.

Joe was a businessman engaged in a Bible study with me. God was doing a great work in His life and Joe was challenged to give His business to the Lord and use it to expand the Father's Kingdom. Soon Joe began to challenge others to do the same. Now he urges businessmen to use their business for Christ. He leads a ministry that challenges men to take back the major cultural influencers in the community: the art culture, the business world, the sports arena, the educational system, the religious systems, and the political realm. Joe is bearing amazing fruit as he makes himself available to the Lord.

Bob is another successful businessman. Bob wanted to sell his business after growing it for twenty-five years. But God got ahold of Bob's life in a fresh way, and Bob began to see that staying in business and leveraging the gifts God had given him could make a Kingdom impact. Now Bob works to give. He and his wife live frugally but give generously. All over the world, Bob and his wife have impacted the lives of young men and women through their generous giving. Many missionaries are on the field because Bob and his wife help send them. They live a Chair 4 lifestyle using the gifts God has given them. And all over the world disciples are being made because of their hard work.

I could tell so many other stories. The names of many different people are flooding into my mind—simple people who serve an amazing God. Using their unique gifts God has given them, they are making disciples who can make disciples. And God is using them to make a multiplying impact on many others.

THE NEEDS OF GOD'S "FRIENDS"

Moving into Chair 4 brings unique needs into a person's life and ministry. God often calls a Chair 4 person to unique ministry situations. Perhaps it's turning a youth group into a youth ministry that knows how to make disciples. Or helping a women's group become focused on making disciple-makers. A Chair 4 person is no longer content with just leading Bible studies or being involved in church activities. They come to understand the mission of Jesus and the mission given to us, and they too want to experience Him fully. They too want to experience disciple-making and building a movement of multiplication.

For over twenty-five years I led a ministry called Sonlife. Our mission was "restoring to the heart of the local church a passion for Great Commission and Great Commandment living." For the first twelve years we trained youth pastors to develop disciple-making ministries. This was both a joy and challenge. Moving from youth groups to a disciple-making youth ministry often created much fruit but also many challenges. Gone were the days of babysitting church kids or social outings with no greater meaning. Everything became focused on disciple-making and, like in the days of Jesus, this upset some people. Many youth pastors became targets for upset parents who wanted the youth pastor simply to babysit and entertain their children.

Leading a disciple-making ministry can bring attacks from many directions, and the Chair 4 person needs to know how to defend himself or herself. Satan doesn't mind if we just stay busy with church activities. But when we begin to reach the lost, grow new believers, and then equip them to go and repeat the process, we become targets for the enemy.[2]

As strange as it may seem, I have found again and again that Chair 4 disciple-makers become almost the enemy of the traditional church system. Let me tell you about Tom. Tom began to really grow in his faith and developed a deep burden for his neighbors who did not know Christ. Tom began to pray for them, invite them into a neighborhood Bible study, and then see them come to Christ and begin to reach out to their friends. In time, several Bible studies were started, and many of the people wanted to meet together, not only to study the Bible, but to be baptized and to worship together. Most were unchurched and had no contact with an established church. So Tom began a neighborhood worship gathering at the local community center.

Word got back to the church leadership and they called Tom in. Why wasn't he supportive of the church's meetings? Why didn't he bring his neighbors to the church services? Tom tried to explain that he had invited them, but that they felt threatened by a traditional church and knew few people in the church. The leadership criticized Tom for not being a team player.

In reality, Tom should have been commissioned to go and reach his neighborhood, maybe even plant a new church. Perhaps this local gathering could have sent some people out to help, deepening their maturity and development. But instead Tom began to be labeled as "trying to do his own thing." The truth is, Tom was just concerned for making disciples where he lived and helping them make disciples of their family and friends.

Tom's is just one of many stories I could tell you. Annette was never supported by churches in her vision to build a hospital. "That is not one of our church's priorities," Annette was told. Bob was questioned for not supporting the missions programs of his church when he chose to support multiple different ministries, which he saw as fruitful in making disciples. Joe was questioned for focusing so much on reaching leaders outside of the church and spending too much time in the political and cultural realm. Questions and criticism can come from many directions, and this is only understandable. But it is often most painful when it comes from within. Jesus experienced push back from those who should have been most receptive to His message and we will often face the same. In John 15 Jesus reminds His disciples, "If the world hates you, keep in mind that it hated me first" (15:18). "A servant is not greater than his master. If they persecuted me, they will persecute you also" (15:20).

The person who moves into Chair 4 and has learned the lessons of Chairs 1 through 3 now knows God can do something amazingly different through his or her life. This person knows how to work and serve, has a heart for evangelism and discipleship, and knows how to make disciples. For this reason, God often calls them to a unique task that He has on His heart. God uses Chair 4 people to launch totally new ministries, often in totally new ways. People like Dawson Trotman, launching a ministry to military men (the Navigators), or Bill Bright being burdened for the college campus (Campus Crusade for Christ), or Jim Rayburn, passionate about reaching unchurched teens (Young Life). God knows He has people whose hearts belong to Him and who follow His voice, and thus He freely uses them in new ventures. This is how multiplication begins on a massive scale—not just the multiplication of disciples, but also the multiplication of discipling ministries.

I love finding these people and helping them succeed. They become powerful tools in the hand of God. They often need help defining the mission God has given them, clarifying the values of the new ministry, and then establishing faith and work goals coupled with an effective ministry/business plan. They often have to learn to navigate the misunderstandings that come from traditional church systems. And while many traditional churches see these people as a threat, they should be championed, commissioned, supported, and sent out. When a church truly gets effective in making disciple-makers, these types of people multiply.

More often than not, they multiply far beyond the church's ability to support them financially. But there are multiple levels of support. They can be championed from the pulpit as disciple-makers. They can be commissioned and sent out with prayers and perhaps even with other disciple-makers to launch new ministries or plant new churches.

PRINCIPLES FOR MINISTRY TO PEOPLE IN CHAIR 4

1) Our goal is multiplication. Never forget: our goal is multiplication. We want to reach new people (Chair 1), see them grow (Chair 2), equip them as workers (Chair 3), and then send them out to launch new ministries (Chair 4). Multiplication is our goal. We must send them out. We want them to leave. We want them to start their own families. We want them to "go and bear fruit."

This is almost counterintuitive to the American way. In America we value getting bigger, adding more people, growing in the number of activities and options. Growth is good. But multiplication is much better. Look at it this way. If you attended a church of 100 people and it grows by a healthy conversion growth rate of ten percent a year, your church would double in size every 7.2 years. Within about thirty years, it would grow to include 1,600 people (if no one left or died). But if that same church of 100 people each multiplied themselves into one other disciple who could also make disciples, and if you allowed each disciple three years to reproduce themselves, in ten years that church of 100 would become a church of 1,000. In twenty years it would grow to more than 10,000 people. And in thirty years, this same church would now be over 100,000 people strong, all through the power of multiplication. No wonder Jesus focused on multiplication instead of growth!

2) Chair 4 people may look like the enemy. Because these people are passionate about reaching new people groups and are secure in their walk with the Lord, God often calls them to new adventures and new tasks. Instead of hanging around and helping out, they are often out launching new ministries or recruiting others to do the same. To an established church, sadly, this can look like the competition. In reality, this is what bearing "much fruit" looks like. We need to help these people clarify their calling, define their mission, establish their values, and then commission them to be sent out. We need to prayerfully keep in touch and hear stories of how God is working, sharing in the fruit of multiplication. Rather than seeing these people as our competition, we need to help them clarify God's call on their life, and rejoice with them in the multiplication of God's Kingdom.

3) Chair 4 people may look very different from each other. While disciple-making follows a natural and organic process of growth and development, the end product can often look quite different. Because of how God gifts various people, some Chair 4 people may be called to plant a church, others to serve as youth pastor or men's ministry pastor in the local church. Some may be called to launch a homeless shelter or work with prostitutes in the red light district. Some may be called to launch a food bank or provide used clothing to the needy. Some may be called to reach the poorest of the poor. Some may have a passion to reach the educational community and others may have a passion for the business community. Each will vary and this is how God expands His Kingdom. They will have a variety of ministry callings, but they share a common passion. Reach the lost seeker, grow the new believer, equip the young worker, and then send out the proven disciple-maker. This one mission has multiple results.

After thirty years of training in disciple-making, I'm often asked what is my best description of what a healthy disciple-making ministry looks like? My answer is simple: it is messy. This is the case simply because a healthy disciple-making ministry is constantly seeing new people come to Christ, and spiritual babies bring many dirty diapers. As these babies begin to grow into young men and women in the Lord, they begin to see how much of a mess they really are. As they see sin in themselves and begin to deal with it honestly and faithfully—well, that's messy too. As we become effective at teaming up with others and reaching out, we begin to build our own family of disciples. And as they grow and become disciple-makers, we move from parenting to grandparenting, carrying the burdens and joys that come with a growing family of disciples. This too is messy. To be honest, I'd rather have this type of mess than the mess that you have when disciple-making is not happening. This often just results in ingrown Churchianity, rather than real Christianity. I'd much rather have the mess of multiplication with lots of new seekers, new spiritual babies, growing disciples, and then multiplying disciple-makers.

The growth from Chair 1 to Chair 4 is God's great design for disciples of Jesus. This development can only be accomplished in the power of the Holy Spirit. There are a few obstacles to growth at each point in this journey that the disciple-maker should be aware of. Those obstacles are the focus of the next two chapters.

PONDERINGS

1. From your perspective, what are some of the challenges that come with parenting? How might these same challenges apply in "spiritual" parenting?

_____

_____

_____

_____

2. How does family living differ from just living alone? What are the advantages of family living, and what are the difficulties?

_____

_____

_____

_____

3. Read 1 John 2:12–14. How do fathers, children, and young men differ in what they have accomplished?

_____

_____

_____

_____

CHAPTER NINE

Sticking Points (Mark 4)

My classmates in our little redbrick country school were known for playing practical jokes on people. Our favorite prank was placing tacks on our teacher's chair and waiting for her to jump with pain after sitting down. Our next favorite joke was smearing clear Elmer's glue on one another's chairs. When someone sat on the glue, it would start to dry, and then when they tried to stand up they would stick to the chair. If they pulled too hard they could tear their jeans, but in most cases, they just found the chair difficult to slide out of. They were stuck. In a similar way, I have found that each of the four chairs in our discipling metaphor has certain sticking points that can make it very difficult to get out of the chair and move to the next level.

In Mark 4, Jesus delivers to His disciples the parable of the soils. The parable addresses several of these sticking points. A farmer sows seed broadly. Some of the seed falls on the hardened path, and the birds of the air swoop down and take it away. Other seeds fall on the rocky places, only to spring up quickly but then die out because the new plants lack roots. Some seed falls among the thorns, only to later be choked out by them. Finally, some seed falls on good soil, growing to multiply thirty, sixty, and even a hundred times. There are several ways to interpret this parable, but I want to look at the story from the perspective of the farmer seeking to bring in a harvest.[1]

SEED SOWN ALONG THE PATH

In any farming community, and especially in rocky Israel, seed sown along a hardened rocky path has little hope of becoming fruitful. The soil is hard, uncultivated, and not receptive to outside seed. In this parable the birds of the air (a metaphor for Satan) come along and steal the seed that is sown on the hard ground. The seed has no chance to begin to grow. Luke 8:12 tells us plainly the condition of this person: "the devil comes and takes away the word from their hearts, so that they may not believe and be saved." As we are told in John 12:24, a kernel of wheat must fall to the ground and die before it can begin to multiply. In this metaphor, the seed does not have this chance to take up root in a person's life, and thus the person never comes to the truth. This is a Chair 1 person who hears the Word but does not have a receptive heart. As a result they never move beyond Chair 1 and remain stuck in that position.

The solution to this problem is breaking up the hardened ground. Isaiah 28:23–29 addresses this condition. "Listen and hear my voice; pay attention and hear what I say. When a farmer plows for planting, does he plow continually? Does he keep on breaking up and working the soil?" (vv. 23–24). Four times in this text we are told to "listen," "pay attention," "hear what I say," or "hear my voice." Do you think God is trying to tell us something?

For a farmer to have receptive soil, he must do the hard work of cultivating the soil. It is during this task when the tractor or animal pulling the plow works the hardest. When a tractor is plowing, dark smoke pours from the exhaust pipe as the engine strains. But that's just the first step. After plowing, you then disk the soil with sharp blades to further separate the freshly plowed furrows. My job as a child during this process was to pick up the larger stones that were overturned in the soil. All of this was necessary before we could plant the seeds. Breaking up the hardened ground takes time and energy.

In the same way, if friendships and relationships are not cultivated before the seed is sown, in many cases the birds of the air come and take away the seed. Becoming a "friend of sinners" like Jesus did, begins this process. The cultivating of relationships, the preparation of the soil, the removing of the larger rocks, and the careful sowing of the seed all help move people from Chair 1 to Chair 2.

SEED SOWN ON ROCKY PLACES

Nick was a good friend at college. When I had the privilege of sharing the Good News with Nick, he was quick to respond. Much like myself, he was searching for forgiveness and knew that he had failed God in many respects. He knew he needed meaning in life beyond weekend parties and a full-time job. When Nick heard that God had a wonderful plan for his life and offered the forgiveness and meaning he sought, Nick was quick to turn from sin and invited Christ to lead his life.

Immediately Nick was filled with a true sense of joy and purpose and began to share this with his family and friends at college. However, Nick failed to be a true disciple (learner) and go deeper in the Scriptures. For a seed to germinate, it needs to put its roots down so it can go deep, gather nutrients from the soil, and be able to withstand the storms that come. "Being rooted and built up" is essential for long-term living and the multiplication of fruit (Colossians 2:7). But Nick's faith never developed deep roots. As he faced challenging questions, he was unable to give adequate answers. His faith began to diminish and as a result, his feelings of joy and meaning began to wane. Soon Nick experienced real persecution because of his stand alongside of the Word of God and Nick found himself unable to adequately handle himself. Eventually Nick fell away from the faith.

Jesus describes Nick's situation in His parable. "Others, like seed sown on rocky places, hear the word and at once receive it with joy," Jesus explains. "But since they have no root, they last only a short time. When trouble or persecution comes because of the word, they quickly fall away" (Mark 4:16–17). Trouble and persecution will come; it is not a matter of "if" but "when."

One morning my wife said to me, "Have you looked out the front window and seen what happened to our beautiful flowering tree?" I looked out the window in shock. Our beautiful ten-foot flowering tree had fallen over and was lying on the sidewalk. We asked a professional landscaper for his opinion on what happened. He told us that under the flowering tree is a solid rock. The tree has roots, but they are shallow and unable to go deep. The tree may last awhile, but in time it will probably die. It simply doesn't have a good root system from which to get proper nutrients and with which to stand the pressures of storms that can blow it over.

In the same way, with insufficient roots, a growing believer will never reach the fruit-bearing stage. Any of us trying to disciple new Christians, need to consider carefully the importance of a good root system. Very practically, let me suggest a few things that can be done:

Discuss. Take your new Christ-follower and study this parable of the soils. Ask them how much fruit they want to bear. Discuss what keeps people from growing deep roots. Share some of the issues you faced as you began to grow in the Word and began to share your faith. Allow your disciple to learn from you.

Study. Spend a good deal of time studying who they are in Christ and what Christ has done for them. Neal Anderson's ministry, Freedom in Christ, has books and studies on this subject. Sonlife has a simple little booklet called "33 Things that Happened at Salvation." Or you can simply go to Colossians 1–3 or Ephesians 1–3 and study who we are in Christ. Help your disciple put their roots down deep.

Trust. Teach your disciple that living by faith in the power of the Spirit is how we go from victory to victory. Any attempt in our own strength to walk like Christ will only result in failure. As we live a cleansed life, immediately confessing any known sin, we are cleansed from all unrighteousness and can walk in His power. Help your disciple to know how to deal with sin immediately and to walk in the Spirit's power.

Allow. Give your new disciple the freedom to fail. Don't push them too hard or expect maturity too soon. As parents, we need to allow our children to mature in the appropriate time frame, never expecting an infant to be able to run before we teach them to walk.

Pray. As Paul modeled, we must pray for new Christians that "the eyes of your heart may be enlightened in order that you may know the hope to which he has called you, the riches of his glorious inheritance in his holy people" (Ephesians 1:18). Knowing Christ and what He has done for us will always be the basis for our identity. This is a lifelong process of being rooted in Him, a reality that God increasingly reveals to us as we mature. It is this root system that sustains us as we invest our lives for His cause.

SEED SOWN AMONG THORNS

As the parable continues, Jesus identifies at least three additional sticking points. "Still others, like seed sown among thorns, hear the word," Jesus says, "but the worries of this life, the deceitfulness of wealth and the desires for other things come in and choke the word, making it unfruitful."

It is important to realize that in these last two illustrations where there are no roots and no fruit, there is nevertheless some initial growth. The seed has germinated, begins to grow, and is moving toward fruitfulness, but something keeps it from getting there. Three sticking points—worries, wealth, and wants—can all choke out fruitfulness. All of us face worries. All of us face the deceitfulness of wealth. All of face the wants (desires) of life. The question is how do we keep them from choking us out?

Again, how do we practically overcome these sticking points? I suggest just a few very practical considerations:

Discuss. Take time to discuss how each of these challenges affects you and your disciple personally. All of us have different patterns of worry and all of us are influenced differently by the various "wants" of life. We must know ourselves and we must know our disciple if we are going to help them overcome these sticking points.

Discern. How are these issues working out in our life? We all have blind spots, and without the help of godly people around us who care enough to confront us, we may never see those blind spots personally, and thus have a hard time helping others.

Destroy. We need to aggressively tackle any of these thorns that can choke out fruitfulness. It is no coincidence that three out of the four people in this parable do not make it to fruitfulness. And this is because we do not take seriously the issues that Christ clearly warned us about in this passage—worries, wealth, and wants.

Demand. Ask for accountability. Learn to listen to close friends who see your life and can speak into it. Demand of yourself and your disciples accountability for how you are handling your finances. So often all three of these sticking points can easily revolve around money. Demand accountability on tithing first and foremost, as this is God's way of helping us keep these issues in check. Failure to be willing to tithe is usually a clear indicator of these issues having root in a person's life.

If we take this parable at face value, it seems that 75 percent of the people who begin the journey of disciple-making never move into Chair 3 or Chair 4 faithfulness. This is why Jesus said, "the harvest is plentiful but the workers are few." The "workers" are Chair 3 and Chair 4 Christians. Discuss this reality with your disciple and honestly evaluate their commitment. Ask them, Have you made a commitment to moving beyond "no life" (v. 15), "no roots" (v. 17), and "no fruit" (v. 19) to become a thirty, sixty, or one hundredfold fruitful follower (v. 20)?

SEED SOWN ON GOOD SOIL

It is obvious in this parable that the second and third seeds are moving toward fruitful living but never make it because of troubles, persecution, worry, the deceitfulness of wealth, or the desires of life. They begin to grow, but ultimately get stopped before they become fruitful. They stay on the left side of Chair 2 in this metaphor, never making it to multiplication (fruitfulness).

But Jesus goes on and says that, "Others, like seed sown on good soil, hear the word, accept it, and produce a crop—some thirty, some sixty, some a hundred times what was sown" (Mark 4:20). Isn't this where we should all long to be? The multiplication of disciples is totally dependent upon becoming a fruitful disciple ourselves and then helping others do the same! It cannot happen without intentionality, clear teaching, and training. This is what Paul describes in 1 Thessalonians 2:8 when he writes, "We loved you so much, we were delighted to share with you not only the gospel of God but our lives as well." Nurturing a disciple to fruitfulness requires giving care like a "nursing mother" (2:7), a "brother" (2:9), and a "father" (2:11). It demands that we invest our lives in each other.

For years my wife and I loved growing cactus plants in our first apartment. I was a lousy gardener, so I assumed that if water was good, then a lot of water was better. I assumed that if sunlight was good, then lots of sunlight was better. About every six months my wife had to buy new plants. I was killing them as fast as my wife could bring them home! I soon learned that too much water was not good, and the amount of sunlight necessary varies from plant to plant. In time I learned what each plant needed and helped create the proper environment for healthy growth. God gave the increase, but we helped provide the proper environment. And the same is true with helping our disciple to grow. Fruit takes time, and it comes in seasons. A farmer understands this and does all he can to maximize the fruit-bearing. While we cannot make fruit happen, we can create a healthy environment for maximum growth to take place. Fruitfulness is not something we can produce. It is a byproduct of abiding in the Vine, Jesus.

FRUIT INSPECTING

Currently I lead a ministry called Global Youth Initiative. We work in more than eighty countries with young leaders who are passionate about creating movements of multiplying disciples. The more I mature, the more I find myself becoming a "fruit inspector." So many try to hang plastic fruit on their Christian life, and from a distance it may look like the real fruit. But a true gardener inspects the fruit up close, and knows the difference. It is important as we disciple new believers that we inspect their spiritual fruit. Biblically fruit is identified in at least three areas. The first is character, the fruit of the Spirit (Galatians 5:22–23). Am I seeing these qualities present and growing in my disciple's life? The second is conduct, or the fruits of service and righteousness (Philippians 1:11). Is the disciple growing in his or her acts of service toward others? The third is converts, or new disciples (Romans 1:13). Is anyone coming to Christ through the ministry of the disciple? We ask these questions, and inspect the fruit, not out of a critical spirit but out of a deep desire to help younger leaders be sure that true abiding is happening. We need to do this gently and lovingly, with those we are trying to disciple.

A number of years ago I discussed this parable of the soils with a young man I was discipling. Tom was a new youth pastor in Michigan. He had a heart of gold for the things of God. Tom was a simple guy with few gifts that many think are necessary to be a good youth pastor. Tom's greatest gift was his love for people, and Tom just loved the twenty or thirty kids in his ministry. When we discussed the parable of the sower, Tom was quick to say, "I doubt I can become a hundredfold type of fruit bearer, but I'd like to trust God to become a sixty-fold type of guy." For Tom, this meant multiplying his life sixty-fold.

This was over thirty years ago. In my last discussion with Tom a number of years ago, he could identify nearly sixty people who had come through his ministry who now were serving the Lord full-time. That is fruitfulness and endurance, and I'm sure heaven for Tom will be an eternity of finding new stories of how his faithfulness was multiplied through the generations for the Lord's glory.

How fruitful do you want to be? What could you trust God for? In this next chapter, we will continue to look at this subject of fruitfulness, and lay another layer of Scriptures over this 4 chair metaphor.

PONDERINGS

1. Which of these sticking points—worries, wealth, wants—is most challenging for you? Why?

_____

_____

2. What do your children (or disciples) struggle with most?

_____

_____

3. What are some of the benefits of discussing this parable with someone you are discipling?

_____

_____

Visit www.4ChairDiscipling.com for more resources.

CHAPTER TEN

Barriers between Chairs (John 15)

J esus speaks His last words to His disciples in John 15. The events recorded in John 15 come near the end of "the days of Jesus' life on earth" (Hebrews 5:7). They probably occurred after Jesus left the upper room, where He participated in His last Passover meal with His disciples. In John 15 they are headed down to the Garden of Gethsemane where Jesus will be betrayed by Judas.

On the way, as they are passing through a vineyard, Jesus seizes the opportunity to summarize His ultimate plans for His disciples. In this powerfully visual passage, Jesus gives us a picture of His desire for you and me, also, as He speaks of four levels of fruit-bearing: no fruit, fruit, more fruit, and much fruit.

> I am the true vine, and my Father is the gardener. He cuts off every branch in me that bears no fruit, while every branch that does bear fruit he prunes so that it will be even more fruitful. You are already clean because of the word I have spoken to you. Remain in me, as I also remain in you. No branch can bear fruit by itself; it must remain in the vine. Neither can you bear fruit unless you remain in me. I am the vine; you are the branches. If you remain in me and I in you, you will bear much fruit; apart from me you can do nothing. If you do not remain in me, you are like a branch that is thrown away and withers; such branches are picked up, thrown into the fire and burned. If you remain in me and my words remain in you, ask whatever you wish, and it will be done for you. This is to my Father's glory, that you

bear much fruit, showing yourselves to be my disciples. (John 15:1–8)

In this parable, the four levels of fruitfulness correspond to the four chairs. Chair 1 represents "no fruit," as the lost person can do nothing to yield a harvest for God. Chair 2 represents "fruit," because a new believer begins to grow a harvest for the Lord. Chair 3, the worker, represents "more fruit." But Chair 4 represents "much fruit," the disciple-making disciple.

According to Jesus, the Father's ultimate goal for every one of us is to move us to the "much fruit" level, so that we can prove we are His disciples and thus bring Him glory. "By this my Father is glorified," Jesus claims, "that you bear much fruit and so prove to be my disciples" (John 15:8 ESV). However, not every believer ultimately bears much fruit. There is a definite progression of fruit-bearing with some definite barriers between each level. Fortunately, Jesus also exposes barriers that keep us from getting to the next level, and gives His Father's remedy.

BARRIER 1: SIN

The first barrier I see is the barrier of sin. Jesus states, "He [my Father] cuts off every branch in me that bears no fruit" (John 15:2). The word translated "cuts off" is the Greek word *airo*, and it is used over a hundred times in the New Testament. But only here is it translated "cuts off." The word literally means to "lift up" or "move to a different location." In Matthew 9:6, for example, after Jesus heals the paralyzed man, He tells him to *airo* his mat and go home—to lift it up and take it someplace else.

If you ever have the opportunity to visit a vineyard, you will find the vines carefully lifted up and placed on wire trellises. If a gardener sees a vine that has fallen from the trellises, he will lift it up (*airo*) out of the dirt, clean it off if necessary, and place it back in the sunlight so that it can eventually bear fruit. If it is left in the mud, it will become like a branch that withers, and will be thrown in the fire to burn (John 15:6).

The barrier between no fruit and fruit is simply the barrier of sin. Sin causes us to fall out of the sunlight (Son) and into the dirt. If we are left in the dirt, we will shrivel up and become unproductive. But if we are lifted up (*airo*), cleaned off if necessary (Jesus said, "you are already clean"), and placed back into the Son light, then we can move from no fruit to fruit. Jesus makes it clear: we cannot bear fruit apart from Him (John 15:5). And in the same way, we cannot bear fruit if sin is controlling our lives. We must deal with known sin, and then the Lord will cleanse us from "all unrighteousness" (1 John 1:9). Sin is the barrier that keeps us from bearing fruit. Every day spent in sin is a day we fail to bear fruit.

Because of this, it is critical that we teach our disciples how to immediately and completely repent of any known sin. Granted, we all need to repent initially of our sinfulness. But I love what the Christians in Romania call each other—Repenters! For them the Christian life is a life of repenting. Confessing known sin, by faith claiming Christ's cleansing, and then moving forward in the power of the Spirit. This is a Repenters' lifestyle.

This passage raises the question, If someone produces no fruit, are they even a Christian? Some would like to argue that if there is no fruit there must not be any real life. And while there is some truth in this statement, let's be careful about making quick assessments. In this passage, we are told the Gardener cuts off every person (branch) "in me" that bears no fruit. Up to this point in the gospel of John, whenever anyone is referred to being "in me," that person is a Christian. You cannot be in Christ without having Christ in you.

We have to ask ourselves, Has there ever been an hour we have lived in sin and failed to bear fruit? Has there been a day? Or a week? Or a few years? All of us would have to answer yes. You can be in Christ but still have unconfessed sin in your life. It doesn't change our status as a Christian, but it does affect our ability to bear fruit.

The real question, I think, is, Can you be in Christ for a long time and still bear no fruit? To this question I would have to answer no. Because God's clear agenda is to get all of us to the place where we bear fruit, more fruit, and much fruit. And He will do whatever that takes to make this happen. He is jealous for His glory.

Hebrews 12 tells us that as a loving Father, God will take us through a process of discipline in our lives if we fail to deal with sin over the long haul. God's process of correction is gentle. It begins with a rebuke and is followed by discipline (Hebrews 12:5–6). If we still fail to respond to His loving discipline, He will punish us (12:6). Be assured, God will not tolerate sin in His child's life for long. God's agenda for us is holiness, which leads to fruitfulness, and sin keeps us from that. If we never experience the discipline of God, then we are probably not sons of God but sons of this world.

No matter how you interpret the text, sin is a barrier to bearing fruit. For the non-Christian, it is a life of sin. For a Christian, it is a persistent lifestyle of unconfessed sin that the Father will address.

BARRIER 2: GOOD THINGS

Moving from bearing no fruit to bearing fruit (Chair 2) is just the beginning of the Lord's plan for His followers. Jesus goes on to say that "He cuts off every branch in me that does not bear fruit, while every branch that does bear fruit, he prunes so that it will be even more fruitful" (Chair 3) (John 15:2).

Sometimes churches accidentally encourage people to stay in Chair 2. We make the Christian life a La-Z-Boy with cup holders, soft seats, and a footrest. We make Chair 2 so comfortable that no one wants to move on. We challenge people to come and see, but we never challenge them to take the next step. As a result they sit, soak, and eventually begin to sour.

In John 15:2, Jesus explains that the way we go from "fruit" to "more fruit" is through pruning. Simply put, a vine will fail to produce an abundant harvest year after year if not carefully pruned. Pruning is what produces the maximum harvest.

A number of years ago I had the privilege of visiting the Biltmore Estate on 125,000 acres of beautiful woodlands in Asheville, North Carolina. It's the largest home in America, with more than 250 rooms—35 bedrooms, 43 bathrooms, and 65 fireplaces. It boasts a vineyard of over 100 acres. There I had the privilege of meeting the primary caretaker of the vineyard, who had earned his PhD as a horticulturist, with a specialty in pruning. I never knew there was so much to learn about pruning!

According to this horticulturist, one of the most critical times to prune is early in the branch's history. Failure to prune early will result in a weak root system, which can cause the branches to become a tangled web of foliage unable to produce enough sap to bear fruit. If not pruned, a branch will eventually die a premature death. But if pruned carefully, though, its life span and fruitfulness dramatically increases.

A typical young branch will surface ten to twelve buds that can become clusters of grapes. But early on, it will need to be pruned back to two or three buds, in order to produce rich, luscious clusters of grapes. Two or three luscious clusters is preferable to ten or twelve mediocre clusters. Interestingly, the gardener is never closer to the branch than when he is pruning it. Each branch is unique, so each branch needs to be carefully analyzed in order to be pruned most effectively. The gardener scrutinizes each branch, because he knows that an abundant harvest is at stake.

As I think about this process of pruning, several questions surface in my mind about the process of moving from Chair 2 to Chair 3. First, since the barrier to "more fruit" is stuff that must be pruned, who then gets pruned? According to John 15:2 it is *every* branch! You don't have to pray for pruning—it *will* come! Another critical question is, When do you get pruned? Again the answer is found in God's Word. It always comes before the harvest. Hebrews 12:11 tells us that though pruning is a painful experience, "later on, however, it produces a harvest of righteousness." But why do I need pruning? The answer is simple: to be more fruitful. But perhaps the most illuminating question of all is, *What* gets pruned? The answer to this is hard to believe. What gets pruned are not the bad things but the good things. A gardener removes a flower—a good thing—from the branch to make room for fruit. And this is what makes pruning so painful.

Many people struggle with pruning for this very reason. Good things are taken away—a job, a loved one, one's health—but to what end? During these experiences, we may be tempted to question God. We begin to doubt God's goodness and His care. A life that was once peaceful becomes painful. A life of fruitfulness now seems to be falling apart. Faith is replaced with doubt. And unfortunately at this stage of the process, many choose to go back into Chair 2. It is too painful to continue in this pruning, so people simply slip back into Chair 2. We're comfortable with that lifestyle. We know what to expect.

Hebrews 10–12 speaks to this journey from Chair 2 to Chair 3. It is addressed to Christians who were enduring great suffering—being thrown in prison, losing their property, and comforting others who had experienced the same. The writer of Hebrews encourages his readers in the midst of this pruning not to "throw away your confidence; it will be richly rewarded" (10:35). Persevere so that you can receive the harvest (10:36). Don't shrink back; lean into this tough time with faith (10:38–39).

Pruning is a struggle. It is painful. It demands submission and a willing spirit, but it is ultimately for "our good" (Hebrews 12:4–10). Even so, it causes us to be weary and weakened and seemingly unstable (12:13), causing us to need a level path and encouragement. In the midst of this pruning we need God's grace. The Bible's warning is very clear. "See to it that no one falls short of the grace of God and that no bitter root grows up to cause trouble and defile many" (12:15). If at any time in this painful process we see that bitterness springing up, we must get on our knees and ask God where we missed His grace.

Some of the most veteran disciple-makers in history, men like Leroy Eims, Dawson Trotman, Robert Coleman, or Carl Wilson, have clearly stated the number one destroyer of disciples is bitterness. Making it through Chair 3 is tough, and bitterness can settle in if we fail to allow His Spirit to give us His grace. Once bitter, we become victims to unfruitfulness. But God's grace is sufficient, and He again and again will help us to move from "grace to grace" as we grow in fruitfulness.

Chair 3 barriers are not easy to break through. But overcoming them brings great joy and an increasing harvest. We begin to share in both the "power of his resurrection, and participation in his sufferings" (Philippians 3:10). And the only way I know to get to Chair 4 is through the rich lessons associated with going through the barriers of Chair 3.

BARRIER 3: SATISFACTION

Sitting in Chair 3 is a position of more fruit. Those who are not dismayed by the process of pruning can become caught up with the joy of the harvest. We can become satisfied with all the fruit. We are busy enjoying the increased fruit that we are experiencing. But our satisfaction still isn't the goal of our journey. Jesus makes clear that His goal in each of our lives is to get all of us to Chair 4 and so prove to be His disciples (John 15:8).

Something amazing happens in Chair 4 that hasn't happened before. The "much fruit" is so abundant that everyone who looks at our life knows without a doubt it is God who is reaping the harvest! They know us too well. They know we aren't capable of this! It must be God who is doing it! And because of this, He is glorified (John 15:8).

Eight different times in John 15, Jesus uses a powerful word picture that gives us the key breakthrough found between Chair 3 and Chair 4. While I'm suggesting that often the barrier is our satisfaction with more fruit, the breakthrough is the simple phrase *meno*, a Greek word translated as "remain" in the New International Version of the Bible. Elsewhere *meno* is translated as "abide" or "dwell," "continue" or "tarry." It is a beautifully rich word that means, in this context, to "make Jesus our permanent dwelling place." I love how the psalmist says it: "Whoever dwells in the shelter of the Most High will rest in the shadow of the Almighty" (Psalm 91:1). Dwelling in Christ, making Him our permanent dwelling place, brings great rest and security. It is a lifestyle that needs to be cultivated and can only be learned over time. It is a sign of maturity, a sign of Chair 4 living. It produces much fruit—not because of who we are, but because of what He can do through us.

In breaking this barrier, we become a true friend of God. No longer performing, we settle with a balance between striving and resting. Paul describes this balance in these terms: "To this end I strenuously contend with all the energy Christ so powerfully works in me" (Colossians 1:29). God gets glorified as we rest in Him.

PONDERINGS

1. What aspect of this chapter is most interesting to you?

_____

_____

_____

2. Why would it be easy to settle into the "more fruit" chair?

_____

_____

_____

3. Look up the passages mentioned under "fruit" and discuss your
   observations about what fruit looks like.

_____

_____

_____

CHAPTER ELEVEN

Full-Orbed
Disciple-Making

We have defined the process of making disciples in this book based upon four challenges given by Jesus to His disciples. Jesus understood the developmental process and clearly lived on mission in the task of making disciples who could make disciples. At the end of His life and ministry, He told His disciples to "go and make disciples of all nations," following the pattern He gave them.

We began by demonstrating that in order to understand disciple-making according to the pattern of Jesus, we must fully understand the humanity of Jesus. Only if we truly believe that He was fully human, just as we are fully human, will we understand that He lived His life as a model for us to imitate. We are to think and act just like Jesus, learning to walk as He walked following the pattern He gave us.

In the first challenge (Chair 1), Jesus simply invites curious seekers to "come and see." He spends a couple of hours with them, explaining to them that He was the Messiah and pointing them to the Scriptures that revealed Himself. Andrew burst out of that meeting and went immediately to his brother Peter saying, "We have found the Messiah" (John 1:41).

In the second challenge (Chair 2), Jesus goes to Philip and says, "follow me," which was an invitation to come and learn from Him. Philip immediately went and found Nathaneal, and together they spent time with Jesus and the other initial disciples. For several months, they spent time with Jesus and learned from Him (John 3:22).

In the third challenge (Chair 3), eighteen months into the ministry of Christ, Jesus chose five individuals whom He challenged to, "follow me, and I will make you fishers of men." This challenge involved specific training and a major investment of time and energy from Jesus. That investment equipped them to reproduce this life of disciple-making into others.

In the fourth challenge (Chair 4), toward the very end of His ministry, Jesus told the disciples, You did not choose Me, but I chose you and appointed you to "go and bear fruit, fruit that will last." After teaching them how to walk as He walked, committed to His values and priorities, He finally sent them to do what Jesus modeled for them. "Just as My Father has sent Me, so I am sending you," Jesus explained. You are now sent ones. Go and live on mission!

In this 4 Chair metaphor, we have aligned the four chairs in a linear row that reflects the developmental process of walking through the four-year ministry of Jesus. There is a clear developmental process of moving from a seeker, to a child, to a young man, and then a parent. Understanding this process can be helpful as we seek to mature others into Christlikeness. In this last chapter, there is another dimension that needs to be mentioned to be true to the whole of the New Testament.

We have looked at a linear model of disciple-making, to help us understand and reflect upon the developmental process of Jesus in making His disciples. There are great strengths to a linear approach, as much natural growth and development models a linear and organic approach. Growth does happen in defined stages. But let me now give you an additional perspective to consider. The term "disciple" is used more than 250 times in the Gospels. It's not an unusual term or concept, certainly not one unique to Jesus. John had disciples, the Pharisees had disciples, and Jesus had disciples. In the Old Testament and in the Gospels, disciple-making tended to be a top-down system. A disciple knew he wasn't like his teacher, and so a disciple (learner) would follow closely and try to learn everything the discipler knew. One person, the teacher, knew the information the learner wanted to learn. *If you want to know what I know, come and I will teach you what I have experienced.* This is the way practically all learning took place in the time of Jesus.

It is very interesting, then, that after Acts 21:16, the term "disciple" disappears. It is particularly strange, considering we are commanded in the Great Commission to "go and make disciples." A number of different terms begin to replace the term "disciple" in Acts, terms such as "followers of the Way" (Acts 22:4, 24:14) or "Christians" (Acts 11:26). These were new names describing old realities.

More than simply a change in vocabulary, these changes in terms indicate that Jesus had created a new disciple-making system. In place of the old above-below relationship of the master and student, Jesus established a family environment called the church. Strictly speaking, in Christ's church, there is only one Disciple-Maker—Jesus, the Head of the Church. We are all His disciples. As we follow Him, we call others to imitate us as we imitate Christ (1 Corinthians 11:1).

While there is definitely a linear growth process to learn from, there is another way to lay out the chairs. To visualize this, they need to be placed into a circle around a table. The table symbolizes the nature of Christ's church as a family.

In a family you need parents who love and care for the children. You also need, for energy's sake and purposes of joy, children and young men. We all contribute something different to one another. This is what family is all about. And this is a perfect biblical image of the local church, the family of God.

Disciple-making in the New Testament is best done in the context of the local assembly of believers, the church. Disciple-making, New

Testament style, is not top-down or above-below, but each of us using our gifts to build up one another. Therefore we understand that new believers are valuable and have things to offer. Mature believers have other valuable contributions to offer. Seekers bring valuable questions and seeking hearts, while young men contribute energy, passion, and zeal. Around a table there is sweet fellowship as we live life on mission, learning from each other, growing together, and each sharing our gifts and insight. Maturing together we become more like Christ.

This context is the perfect place to offer my personal definition of disciple-making. It is simply this: "out of my love for God, using my gifts and talents, to multiply the character and priorities of Christ in as many people as possible." This definition has several important parts.

First, it operates on the premise that disciple-making begins with my following the Lord and loving Him with my whole heart, soul, and mind. The Great Commandment is the motive behind the mission. You can only reproduce what you are!

Second, it acknowledges that I can't do everything that is necessary for developing fully trained disciples. I am limited in my gifting and thus I need others. My disciples need the input of others. We need each other.

Third, my goal is not to make a single disciple but to multiply disciple-makers. We invest in such a way that asks those we invest in to turn around and invest in others. We make disciples who can make disciples. This is the principle and process of multiplication.

Fourth, we are dedicated to multiplying Jesus's character and priorities. Our emphasis is not a curriculum or program. Our emphasis is not only Jesus's character and it is not only Jesus's priorities. It is both in balance. *I have found through the years that if you only champion discipling you may not end up talking about Jesus. But if you champion Jesus, you always end up talking about making disciples!* We have to keep these priorities in the right order if we hope to make disciples the way Jesus did. Paul understood this when he said, "I want to know Christ—yes, to know the power of his resurrection and participation in his sufferings, becoming like him in his death" (Philippians 3:10).

Fifth, we are motivated to work with as many people as possible. I work hard to find "reliable people who will also be qualified to teach others" (2 Timothy 2:2). Once I find them, I will move heaven and earth to invest in them. They are worth their weight in gold!

WISDOM FOR THE JOURNEY

Disciple-making is a lifelong journey of becoming like Christ and helping others to do the same. It is the greatest of all journeys and the highest of all callings. Just imagine! We *can do what Jesus did* if we walk as Jesus walked. We can even do greater things because, by His grace, we have a greater amount of time to invest in others and teach them to do the same. A life of learning to "think and act like Jesus" is a life well lived. This kind of life is called Kingdom living.

In his book on disciple-making, Juan Carlos Ortiz writes:

"The Bible says the kingdom of God is like a merchant looking for fine pearls. When he finds a pearl of real worth, he sells everything and buys that pearl.

When man finds Jesus, this pearl costs him everything. Man says, "I want it. How much does it cost?"

The seller says, "It's too dear, too costly."

"How much is it?"

"It costs everything you have."

"I'll buy it!"

"What do you have? "

"I have $10,000 in the bank."

"What else?"

"I have nothing more. That's all I have."

"Have you nothing more?"

"Well, I have a few dollars here in my pocket."

"How many?"

"I'll see: 30, 40, 50, 80, 100, 120—120 dollars."

"That's fine. What else do you have?"

"I have nothing else. That's all."

"Where do you live?"

"I live in my house."

"The house too."

"Then you mean I must live in the garage?"

"Have you a garage, too? That too. What else?"

"Do you mean that I must live in my car, then?"

"Have you a car? That becomes mine. What else?"

"I have nothing else."

"Are you alone in the world?"

"No, I have a wife, two children . . ."

"Your wife and your children too."

" What else?"

"I have nothing else. I am left alone now."

"Oh, you too. Everything. Everything becomes mine: wife, children, house, garage, cars, money, clothing, everything. And, you too.

Now you can use all those things here but don't forget they are mine, as you are. When I need any of the things you are using you must give them to me because now I am the owner."[1]

An exchanged life. His life for ours. A life of fruitfulness in becoming like Jesus, we become pure vessels through whom God can work. Man as God intended man to be. As we continue the journey to become more like Christ, it's important to keep the following reminders in mind.

1) People are at different stages of this process. It is critical that we understand that people are at different stages of the process of disciple-making. That's okay! It is okay to be a baby in Christ—you just don't want to be one for twenty years. It is okay to be a young man and to be learning and experiencing new things. But you don't want to be in that chair for twenty years. Perpetual immaturity is a sign that something is obviously wrong. On the other hand, it is okay to be a mature parent and not enjoy some of the childish things new believers enjoy. But that doesn't mean we should quench the joy in others. Parents must learn to allow our children to enjoy being children. Of course, we must also help them mature beyond childish ways. Maturity means we understand the development process and work with people based on their stage of life and always give them plenty of grace for that stage.

2) The Holy Spirit must be at work in each stage of this journey. Without the Spirit of God working in each of us, we can never grow to understand the depth of who Christ is and what He has done for us. Only the Holy Spirit can convict seekers of their sin and bring them to repentance at the foot of the cross. Only those who are called will seek (John 6:44). I think we all can quickly see how desperately we need God's Spirit to move anyone into Chair 1 as a seeker and then eventually move them to their knees at the Cross in repentance.

But growing in grace and in the knowledge of Christ in Chair 2 also requires the work of the Holy Spirit in our lives. How can a man ever discover the length and breadth and height and depth of God's love for us without the Holy Spirit? We are incapable of knowing God apart from God revealing Himself. And the good news is that God longs to be known and worshipped by us. In fact, that is why we have been created. And yet, without His revealing Himself to us, we are lost in our ability to discover the greatness of our God.

Additionally, none of us can ever move to the worker chair without God helping us become givers and not just takers. We give because of what He has given to us, we serve because of how He has served us, and we love because we understand how much He loved us. We *are* because He is. And without His grace and love, we cannot truly be servants to others. Again, even as workers, we are dependent upon Him.

Finally, none of us can become mature disciple-makers, who now oversee a family of disciples, but for the grace of God. To become a spiritual parent means that God has chosen to work through us to impact others. And this is obviously a work of God . . . His Spirit working in us and through us. As spiritual parents we know better than anyone that "apart from Christ we can do nothing," but "in Christ all things are possible." This too is a work of God!

In every part of this journey toward Christ likeness, we must recognize our dependence on the Spirit of God. We cannot do this in our own power. It is the Son's life in us and through us! "For in him we live and move and have our being" (Acts 17:28).

3) We must be holy people. Any attempt to make disciples the way Jesus did, in our own flesh, will result in failure. Holiness is the ultimate requirement. A life of living in the Spirit, immediately confessing all known sin, and allowing God's Spirit to become our best friend is what holiness is all about.

We cannot be holy apart from His constant cleansing. And holiness is God's agenda for each of us, for as we mature we move from grace to grace and become more like Him. As we mature, we should become better and better at multiplying in others the character and priorities of Christ. Every part of this disciple-making journey requires the disciple-maker to be dependent upon the Holy Spirit and pure in their walk with the Lord. The true disciple-maker is being made into a disciple at the same time He is helping others to become disciples. We follow Him as we actively challenge others to follow Him.

This requires holy living. We reproduce what we are.

FINDING YOUR PLACE ON THE ROAD

In which chair do you find yourself sitting most consistently today? What is the next step you need to take? Who can help you take that next step and move to that next level of maturity in fruitfulness?

Romans 12:3 gives us some very good counsel, "For by the grace given me I say to every one of you: Do not think of yourself more highly than you ought, but rather think of yourself with sober judgment, in accordance with the faith God has distributed to each of you." Paul goes on to say that each of us has certain gifts and these gifts have been given to us for the common good of others.

Pride is not thinking highly of yourself. Pride is thinking "more highly of yourself than you ought." We are encouraged to take a serious inventory of our life and fruitfulness and use our life to serve others and make disciple-makers. No matter who you are, you can invest in others. No matter how much you know or have experienced, there are others from whom you can learn. Don't get off the journey of disciple-making. It is your calling. It is your mission. Live on mission, no matter what your stage of life or ministry. Allow God to use you to make a difference in others.

Our preaching pastors preached a three-week series entitled, "I Want Names!" Our church's vision is to "Be a praying church, that reaches out and challenges everyone to follow Jesus completely." The three messages were on praying, reaching, and challenging. After each excellent message, the pastors said, "We want names!" They encouraged people to write down names and hand them in or post them on the church bulletin board. Who are you praying for? Who are you reaching out to? Who are you challenging to follow Jesus completely?

In the same way, I want names! Where are your disciples? Who are you investing in? I know you may be uncomfortable calling anyone your "disciple." But that doesn't mean you can't identify someone in whom you are intentionally investing to help them mature in their relationship with Christ. Give me names!

One of the joys of leading Global Youth Initiative is the privilege of working with young disciple-makers all over the globe. A few years ago I had the privilege of leading a four-day training on the life of Christ with over 400 young Indian leaders. The criteria for being able to come to this event was that you had to have at least four generations of disciples and be able to show their names. We expected 100 young leaders to sign up. But more than 400 arrived before we finally cut off registrations. For four days, eight hours a day, I taught on the life of Christ— and they still wanted more!

One of my fondest memories of this experience was that almost every young disciple-maker there, when they came and introduced themselves to me, each brought cell phone pictures of their disciples. Their greatest joy and their greatest identity was rooted in their spiritual children and grandchildren, and even great-great-grandchildren. Who are your disciples? Can you name them? Can you identify them? Asking these questions keeps us focused on the mission we've been called to by our Lord.

Our prayer has simply become that we live out this reality:

I AM A DISCIPLE OF JESUS
I have Holy Spirit Power.
The die has been cast; I have stepped over the line;
The decision has been made; I am a disciple of Jesus.

I won't look back, look up, slow down, back away or be still.

My past is redeemed; my present makes sense;

My future is secure. I am finished and done with sight-walking, Small
*   planning, smooth knees,*

Colorless dreams, tame vision, mundane talking,

Cheap giving and dwarfed goals.

I no longer need preeminence, prosperity,

Position, promotions, plaudits or popularity.

I don't have to be right, first, tops, recognized,

Praised, regarded or rewarded.

I now live by faith, lean on His presence, walk by patience,

Am lifted by prayer, and labor by power.

My face is set; my goal is His Kingdom;

My road is narrow; my way rough,

My guide reliable, my mission clear.

I cannot be bought, compromised, detoured,

Lured away, turned back, deluded or delayed.

I will not flinch in the face of sacrifice,

Hesitate in the presence of adversity,

Negotiate at the table of the enemy,

Ponder at the pool of popularity,

Or meander in the maze of mediocrity.

I will not give up, shut up, let up until I have stayed up,

Stored up, prayed up, preached up for the cause of Christ

I AM A DISCIPLE OF JESUS.

I must go 'til He comes,

Give 'til I drop,

Work 'til He stops me

Complete the task He has given me.

And when He comes for His own,

He will have no problem recognizing me . . .

I AM A DISCIPLE OF JESUS!

PONDERINGS

1. What are the implications of the phrase, "People are at different stages of the journey, and that's okay"?

2. What happens when we try to bear fruit in our own strength, without relying on the Holy Spirit? Can you recall a time when you tried to do just that?

3. Describe "full-orbed discipling" in your own words. How do you view the author's personal definition of disciple-making?

4. Where are you in the journey? What chair do you tend to live in?

Visit www.4ChairDiscipling.com for more resources.

APPENDIX ONE

For Elders and Overseers

Though we have emphasized the four challenges (4 Chairs) of Jesus, we also have to acknowledge in God's design a fifth chair. In the Bible, this person is called the shepherd, elder, bishop, or overseer. Here are the three words:

poimen = shepherd or pastor

presbyteros = elderor presbyter

episcopos = overseer or bishop

These leaders are named in no less than fourteen passages of the New Testament Scriptures that address church leadership and each term is used to highlight a different role.[1] How do we know these three labels are talking about the same persons? Because of how the Scriptures speak of them interchangeably.

In Acts 20:17, 28 the apostle Paul meets with the **elders** from Ephesus. He tells them the Holy Spirit has made them **overseers** and asks them to be **shepherds** of the church of God. In Paul's letter to Titus (1:5–7) he asks his fellow worker to appoint **elders** in every town. Then, as he gives qualities to look for in someone who would be an **elder**, he switches terms and begins to call these qualified people **overseers**. And Peter (1 Peter 5:1–2) gives instructions to the **elders**. He tells them, "Be shepherds of God's flock that is under your care, watching over them . . ." (v. 2).

John 10 clearly portrays the role of a good **shepherd** or good **pastor** (good *poimen*). He knows His sheep and the sheep listen to His voice. He provides and protects them, laying down His life for them if necessary. He is the guardian of their soul and leads them into green pastures. He makes us lie down in green pastures when needed, and He leads us beside quiet waters. He guides us in paths of righteousness for His name's sake. He guards and protects, preparing a meal for us even in the presence of our enemies (Psalm 23). Good shepherds follow the example and leading of the Great Shepherd.

Elder and **presbyter** are the English translations of *presbyteros*. It literally means the elder person, advanced in maturity and life. In the New Testament it referenced those who presided over the assemblies (or churches). The term "elder" implies maturity in experience, someone who is respected by others.

Overseer and **bishop** are our English words for the Greek *episcopos*. This term references a man who is charged with the duty of seeing that things are done by others rightly, as in the oversight of the church issues. First Timothy 3 and Titus 1 list the qualifications for this person. Overseers tend to imply the broader issues of managing the direction, vision, mission, and relationships within the church.

Nowhere are we told to "make" elders or shepherds. The biblical way of obtaining leaders is to choose (Acts 6:3, 15:22), select (Exodus 18:21), designate (Luke 6:13), or appoint (Titus 1:5) them. We are commanded to "make disciples" and then, from among the mature, godly, and proven disciple-makers, we are mandated to choose, select, designate, or appoint leaders as overseers. We are warned to "not be hasty in laying on of hands" (1 Timothy 5:22), for they are being set aside for a great responsibility. Titus 1:7 says that an overseer "manages God's household." That raises an important question. What is God's work?

From my perspective, the answer to that question is clear. God's work is to reflect both the character and priorities of Jesus in and through our lives and ministries. To become more Christlike in every way, "to become mature, attaining to the whole measure of the fullness of Christ" (Ephesians 4:13). And because Jesus was all about "making disciples who could make disciples"—and because we are told to do what He did—shouldn't it be the case that the "work" of the church, the work of God, is furthering the work that Jesus began (Acts 1:1)? If so, we need to make sure that we appoint elders and overseers who are proven disciple-makers, so we can fulfill our calling as the church.

THE PROCESS MODELED

Again, we see this leadership selection process modeled in Jesus's life and ministry. He says "come and see" and then "follow me." Spending time with these initial disciples, Jesus invests in them and after a period of about eighteen months, singles out a few individuals and takes them deeper, saying, "follow me and I will make you fishers of men." After modeling for them several fishing trips and ministry opportunities, Jesus is two and a half years into His ministry. The ministry has multiplied, His cousin John has been put in prison (but not yet killed), and Jesus is leading the movement with a handful of trained disciples.

Before Jesus appointed any leaders over the movement, though, He slipped away and—for the very first time recorded in Scripture—He spent the night in prayer. "When morning came," Luke writes, "he called his disciples to him and chose twelve of them, whom he also designated apostles" (Luke 6:13). Mark adds a word about Jesus's reason for doing this: "that they might be with him, and that he might send them out to preach" (Mark 3:14).

Jesus "appoints" and "designates" His leaders after a night of prayer. These men had been with Jesus from the beginning and were being trained through the modeling of His life and ministry to do what He had been doing. It is two and a half years into His ministry when He appoints them, so to some degree they had proven themselves.

From this point on they would be designated as the Twelve (later the Eleven) and were acknowledged as overseers of the Jesus movement. The very title "apostle" designates a "sent one" and communicates the leadership position they had been given. Even right after His designation of them as apostles, Jesus then preached His famous Sermon on the Mount (Luke 6 or Matt 5–7) that begins with the famous "blessings" and then "curses" (woes). This is the same sermon outline used by Moses in the Old Testament when he appointed Joshua as the leader to take the people into the Promised Land (Deuteronomy

11:26–31). Everyone who was familiar with the Old Testament recognized these men as leaders of this movement. That is why they (the Twelve) began to soon argue about which of them is the greatest leader, and Jesus had to call a leadership team meeting, pull them aside, and talk about servanthood and humility (Luke 9:46 and 22:24).

In Acts 4–6 you see the apostles as leaders of the church. In Acts 6 the apostles select some additional leaders, men full of faith and the Holy Spirit and, as a result, the "number of disciples in Jerusalem increased rapidly, and a large number of priests became obedient to the faith" (6:7). In Acts 11:29–30 appears the first reference to "elders," which indicates a further multiplication of leadership—first the apostles, then the seven, and now elders, Barnabas and Paul, are commissioned in Acts 13:2. By Acts 14:23, these two appointed others with prayer and fasting in each church, just as they had been set apart in Antioch. By Acts 15:2 additional elders are multiplied in Jerusalem, plus two more leaders, Judas and Silas.

In response to internal conflict, you now have the multiplication of two leadership teams (Acts 15:37–38) being sent out . . . Paul with Silas and Barnabas with John Mark.

In Acts 16 and 18 we are introduced to additional disciples who would become leaders . . . Timothy (16:1–2), Priscilla and Acquila (18:18–19), and Apollos (18:24–26). Acts 19–21 continue this multiplication with Erastus (19:22), Sopater, Aristarchus, Secundus, Gaius, Timothy, Tychicus, and Trophimus (20:4, 21:29).

In Acts 20:17 we read of the elders in Ephesus, in Philippians 1:1 we now have overseers and deacons, in 1 Peter 1:1 and 5:1–5 we have Peter with the elders of Pontus, Galatia, Cappodocia, Asia, and Bithynia. In Titus 1:5 Paul instructs Titus to do that which was left undone, and go and "appoint elders in every town."

Throughout the remainder of the New Testament the same process is repeated: seekers are won, new believers are growing, workers are being equipped, and churches are being formed. Elders are then appointed to oversee the multiplication and duplication of this disciple-making process (Titus 1:5).

Within two years the original Twelve trained disciples filled Jerusalem with their teaching (Acts 5:28) and had equipped "multiplying disciples" (Acts 6:7). Within four and a half years they had "multiplying churches" (Acts 9:31). Within nineteen years it was said of them that they "turned the world upside down" (Acts 17:6 KJV), and within twenty-eight years it was said that "the gospel is bearing fruit and growing throughout the world" (Colossians 1:6) and "that has been proclaimed to every creature under heaven" (Colossians 1:23).

Can you imagine what could happen if this was said of your life and ministry? Can you imagine what Jesus meant when He said we can do even greater things if we have faith in Him?

NEEDS OF ELDERS AND OVERSEERS

1) Clarity of vision. With so many needs coming to the leaders of a church, clarity must constantly be communicated. What is the "work of the church"? Are we making disciples who can make disciples? How do our activities help us accomplish our mission? Where are we strong and where are we weak in moving people through the 4 Chairs?

It was encouraging for me when I first took the elders of Southeast Christian Church through the training, that they together in unison said we are good at Chair 1 and 2, but we must strengthen Chairs 3–4. Clarity of vision! Many churches can be good at Chair 2 and somewhat at Chair 3 but are doing very little at Chair 1. As a result they become ingrown, stagnant, and out of touch with the community around them. Overseers are to oversee the work of the church and must constantly, like Jesus, keep a laser focus on the work we have been called to do, to make sure the church is always moving disciples through the disciple-making process.

2) Freedom to lead. Given the responsibility to protect the mission, vision, and values of the church, leaders must be given the freedom to change what needs to be changed and lead where leadership is needed. This demands followers who understand their role of being a disciple-maker—obeying and submitting to their leaders (Hebrews 13:17), praying for them (1 Timothy 2:1–2), and respecting them (Romans 13:7).

So often programs and activities that were begun with a specific purpose no longer are needed or effective in the purpose for which they were started. Programs or activities can become sacred and any attempt to change or adjust sacred programs can be seen as uncaring. We must remember that programs are not sacred. As someone has said, "for goodness' sake, if the horse is dead, dismount!" Only the mission of making disciples through winning the lost (Chair 1), building believers (Chair 2), equipping workers (Chair 3), and sending out proven multipliers (Chair 4) is sacred. Programs come and go but the mission stays the same. Leaders need the freedom to make adjustments as needed. Followers (disciple-makers) need to respect, submit, and obey leaders as they seek what is best in the oversight of the church.

3) Modeling the process. We reproduce what we are. Leaders who tell people to make disciples but don't model and champion the process make it difficult for others to follow. Jesus clearly modeled the process. As the ministry grew larger and larger, Jesus became more and more focused on investing in the few. Within the last year alone, Jesus took a twenty-mile trip northwest over the difficult Upper Galilean Mountains to Tyre and Sidon to spend time with His disciples (Matthew 15:21). Later He went north up to Caesarea Philippi to teach His disciples some powerful lessons (Matthew 16:13) and then take just three of them on a lengthy journey up to the Mount of Transfiguration (Matthew 17) before He sets His face to Jerusalem during His last nine months.

Disciple-making is simply *out of the overflow of my love for God, using my talents and gifts, to multiply the character and priorities of Jesus in as many people as possible*. It is simply the "imparting of my life to others" (1 Thessalonians 2:8). Leaders must model this process! They must love God, love people, use their gifts, impart their life, and champion being like Jesus in both His character and priorities. If leaders fail to live this lifestyle and own these values, it will be very difficult for the church to do the same. You reproduce what you are!

PRINCIPLES FOR LEADERSHIP SELECTION

Many principles could be identified in this section on leadership, but let me give just one for our present purposes: you don't need a lot of leaders. Leadership is my top ministry gift, and I believe I understand this gift and calling. And because of this, I often swim upstream when I make this statement, but I firmly believe you don't need a lot of leaders. You just need the right ones! Jesus only had twelve. And they were all He needed. So many want to make the focus of ministry as leadership development. But nowhere does the Scripture say to make leaders. Our mandate is to make disciples, and there is a difference!

I'm convinced that if we keep our laser focus upon making disciples, we will have more leaders than we know what to do with. The work of ministry is disciple-making. As we keep our focus on this, and then our ministry grows, God will gift faithful men and make them able to equip others. This is the leadership calling.

Leadership is a gift and a calling. Second Timothy 2:2, which many use as only a discipling text, is really in the context of leadership living. Paul writes to Timothy and tells him to find and appoint reliable men who have proven themselves "faithful and able" to teach others also. Faithfulness connotes a proven mature lifestyle. Able connotes an innate ability from the Lord. Faithful and able.

So often, especially in America, we communicate that the goal of the Christian life is to become a positional leader. This is more the American culture than the biblical mandate. In fact, the opposite is true. Our calling is to become a servant, a relational and loving disciple-maker. Paul calls it being a "slave" of the Lord Jesus Christ. When we verbally or nonverbally communicate that our end goal is positional leadership, we then encourage people to pursue that position. If everyone wants to be a leader, or we call everyone a leader, then in reality no one is.

My wife doesn't have natural leadership gifts (even though she has led our three daughters extremely well). But my wife is a godly woman who is passionate about investing in others and making disciples. At one point in our early marriage, because of her fruitfulness in helping other women, she was asked to lead the women's ministry. Without understanding her strengths clearly, I encouraged her to do so, as I had assumed the ultimate of the Christian life was positional leadership.

This role almost did my wife in. She hated it. She did not want to be the leader. She just wanted to serve women and help some other leader. Within six months I saw the error of my encouragement to take the leadership, and she graciously stepped down. Leadership is not the ultimate goal. Servanthood is. She was most effective at being allowed to be fruitful at Chair 4 living.

APPENDIX TWO

Building a Disciple-
Making Ministry

In this book, we have looked at the life of Christ through the lens of a new person who wants to become a Christ-follower. The process is modeled in the progressive journey of the 4 Chairs ("come and see," "follow me," "follow me and fish for men," and "go and bear fruit"). This process can be simplified as win, build, equip, and then multiply.

But there is another way to exegete the life of Christ. We could look at Christ's life and ministry through how Jesus, as a leader, built a movement of disciple-makers. Rather than looking at Jesus through the lens of a follower, what if we looked at how Jesus created a ministry of multiplying disciples as a leader? Jesus's strategy as a leader, who is entering into what His Father was already doing through John the Baptist, now follows a different pattern. The pattern can be summarized as build, equip, win, and then multiply. The slight difference between "win, build, equip, and multiply" and "build, equip, win, and multiply" is a critical one for leadership in developing a movement of multiplying disciples.

For over twenty-five years I led Sonlife Ministries, a ministry with the unique calling of seeking to exegete how Jesus, as a leader, developed a movement of multiplying disciples.[1] And building a disciple-making ministry is different than just making a disciple. Especially if you have been placed as a leader over a group of believers who have never been challenged to imitate Christ in terms of making disciples.

I'd like to present a simple overview of five phases in Christ's ministry, showing how He created a movement of multiplication. I will briefly describe what this looked like in Christ's life and then identify a few implications for ministry leadership.

PHASE 1: PREPARATION PERIOD

Jesus spent the first thirty years of His life preparing for the ministry His Father had for Him. In Luke 1 and 2 we read about the "baby Jesus" and then the "boy Jesus" who "increased in wisdom and stature, in favor with God and man." Scripture tells us that Jesus was fully God (Colossians 1:15) and fully human (Hebrews 2:14,17). In Philippians 2:5–11 we gain a small glimpse into this mystery of God taking on flesh. In order for the humanity of Jesus to be "like us in every way," Jesus chose to temporarily veil His deity so that His humanity could be fully expressed. He chose to give up the independent use of His deity so that His humanity could find full expression.

The implications of this for leaders are profound. Being fully human, Jesus did not always know the next step to take, but He knew where to get the next step. Jesus was not downloaded as a little baby with all biblical data. He had to study the Scriptures. Jesus learned faith and obedience. In this way, and as the second and perfect Adam, Jesus gave us a ministry model and then told us to do exactly what He did. He was man as God intended man to be.

Early in His ministry Jesus clearly settled the issue of purpose. After studying the Scriptures concerning Himself, after seasons of prayer and seeking His Father's will, Jesus understood the purpose of His life. Early in His ministry in His hometown of Nazareth, Jesus proclaimed His mission (Luke 5). Toward the end of His ministry, in the Upper Room, He stated with confidence in His prayer to His Father "I have brought you glory on earth by finishing the work you gave me to do" (John 17:4).

What was the mission of Christ? What was the "work" He completed? The work Jesus spoke of in John 17 was the making of disciples who could make disciples. As a leader, Jesus's mission was not so much to reach the world as it was to make disciples capable of reaching the world. He then told us to do what He did—to make disciple-makers in

every nation who could create and sustain this movement of multiplication. And He prepared Himself well for that calling for thirty years.

PHASE 2: MINISTRY FOUNDATIONS

Christ's primary agenda during the first half of His ministry was
to lay a solid foundation for a future movement of multiplication. The
first half of Jesus's ministry was spent in the Judean wilderness. He
performed only two recorded miracles, challenged five individuals to
"come and see" and "follow me," and primarily spent time with His initial followers. In comparison to the last half of Christ's three and half
years of ministry, the first half was relatively uneventful.

Nevertheless, during this time Jesus focused on six clear foundational priorities. These are discussed in detail in chapter two, but allow
me to summarize them here.

First, He was dependent upon the Holy Spirit entirely. Second,
He placed a high priority on prayer, slipping away to pray more than
forty-five times in the Gospels. Third, He prioritized obedience to a
Kingdom agenda. Obedience is God's love language. Jesus claimed, "I
only do what pleases my Father." Fourth, the Scriptures were central to
all of life and ministry for Jesus. More than eighty times Christ quoted
from the Old Testament. He knew the Word of God and used the Word
of God. Fifth, Jesus constantly exalted His Father with statements
like "everything you have given me comes from you" (John 17:7), and
"everything that I learned from my Father I have made known to you"
(John 15:15), "but the Father who sent me commanded me to say all
that I have spoken . . . for whatever I say is just what the Father has told
me to say" (John 12:49–50). Jesus was reverently submissive to His
Father (Hebrews 5:7). Finally, Jesus intentionally developed loving,
caring relationships with His disciples and the people around Him.
Jesus "spent time with them" (John 3:22), poured His life into them
as a friend, and modeled living with integrity. These six foundational
priorities—the **Holy Spirit**, **P**rayer, **O**bedience, the **W**ord, **E**xalting
the Father, and **R**elationships—are truly the source of Holy Spirit
POWER![2]

PHASE 3: MINISTRY TRAINING

After Christ's first year and three quarters of ministry, His ministry changes. He now challenges five individuals to go deeper with Him. Earlier Jesus said, "Come and you will see" (John 1:39), and then "Follow me" (John 1:43) and now Jesus changes that challenge to "Follow me and I will send you out to fish for people" (Matthew 4:19). Jesus challenged James, John, Simon, Andrew, and later Matthew, to become a part of His first ministry team. He challenged them early on to become multipliers.

This team is not yet the Twelve apostles. They are workers, not yet leaders at this stage of their life. He saw their hearts and potential for future ministry impact. They were **AFTeR** more—Available (Luke 5:1–3), Faithful (Luke 5:4–5), Teachable (Luke 5:6–10a), and Responsive to His leadership (Luke 5:10b–11). Over the next two years, as Christ prioritizes these workers and others who joined them, these workers grow in number to more than seventy. Jesus surfaced a team and prioritized them, teaching them how to reproduce their lives.

PHASE 4: MULTIPLIED OUTREACH

After selecting His ministry team, Jesus mobilized His team for multiplied outreach. Within a few months Jesus moved to Capernaum (Matthew 4:31), where He performed more than thirty different miracles and more than fifty different creative events with individuals and with the crowds. Jesus's priority was to equip His team to become fishers of men, by giving them experience sharing their faith. He continued modeling outreach personally but began to engage His ministry team more aggressively in the work of evangelism. During this phase the ministry began to expand, with increasing numbers hearing the Good News, so that the "news about him spread all the more" (Luke 5:15).

Beginning in this phase of Jesus's ministry, Jesus focused intensely upon training His disciples to become reproducing "fishers of men." After almost three years of investing in this team, and after sending out the seventy-two disciples two-by-two, Jesus is "full of joy" (Luke 10:21). They are beginning to reproduce what He had built into them. While not yet fully equipped, they were beginning to experience the joy of being used in others' lives.

PHASE 5: MOVEMENT EXPANSION

After two and a half years of investing in His followers and select-ing a core ministry team of disciples who were **AFTeR** more, Jesus now spends a night in prayer and chooses the Twelve as His future leadership team. Jesus chose these apostolic leaders from His base of proven workers. The crowds had expanded and Jesus knew He needed additional leadership to expand the movement. Through the Twelve, Jesus knew that the ministry would continue to multiply. After train-ing them further, Jesus would eventually send them from Judea to Samaria and even the remote parts of the earth. After a year of training His new leaders, Jesus transfers full leadership authority to them (Luke 22:28–30).

By studying the book of Acts, you'll see this new leadership team implementing the same ministry model they learned from Jesus. They were doing what Jesus did. They continued steadfast in the Word and prayer, proclaimed the Good News in Jerusalem, Judea, and Samaria, and continued to win the lost, establish believers, and equip workers. The church multiplied throughout the known world as every believer lived out the Great Commission, with a Great Commandment heart.

Jesus's last promise was that He would be with them always, to the very end of the age (Matthew 28:20). Jesus left them, but the Holy Spirit became the source of "power from on high" that continued the movement of multiplication throughout history (Luke 24:49). Over fifty times the book of Acts records the acts of the Holy Spirit as they empowered and trained leaders and multiplied this movement throughout the then known world. Through the years the movement of Christ has prospered in proportion to our "walking as Jesus walked" in dependence upon that same Holy Spirit. But the single command remains the same: make disciples of all nations.

As we grow our ministries, we need to evaluate them on the basis of a strong Christology. Are we doing what Jesus did by making dis-ciples the way Jesus did? And as leaders, are we leading our ministries into becoming disciple-making movements? Do we and our leadership team clearly understand the disciple-making mission and passion? Have we laid a solid foundation based upon the disciplines of prayerful dependence, obedience, the Word, exalting the Father (worship), and intentional relationships—all of this grounded in the power of the Holy Spirit. Are we identifying and prioritizing the few workers who are **AFTeR** more? Are we modeling and helping our people experience outreach as a lifestyle? Are we developing a leadership team that clearly lives out and oversees our mission of disciple-making? Have we empowered and released those leaders to multiply under the Spirit's leadership? Are we listening well to the Holy Spirit's directions for the next steps in God's Kingdom?

Jesus modeled not only how to make disciples (the 4 Chairs), but for leaders of ministries, He also modeled how to create a movement of multiplying disciples with those whom we are shepherding.

APPENDIX THREE

Graphic Overview

	1	2	3	4
Challenge	Come and See *John 1:39*	Follow Me *John 1:43*	Follow Me... Fish for people *Matt 4:19*	Go and Bear Fruit *John 15:16*
Description	Dead/Lost	Children	Young Men	Father (parent)
Biblical Name	Seeker	Believer	Worker	Disciple-Maker
Biblical Concept	Win	Build	Equip	Multiply
Basic Needs	• Gospel • Answers • Christian friends	• Identity • Explanation • Parenting	• Ministry • Opportunities • Peers	• Wisdom • Other models • Mentors
Skills Needed		• Walk • Talk (w/God & others) • Feed themselves • Clean themselves	• Run • Tell God's story • Feed others • Holy Spirit power	• Endure • Defend truth • Teach Word right • Holy lifestyle
Lasting Fruit	No fruit	Fruit	More fruit	Much fruit
Other Needs	CPR	Milk	Meat	Meat
Further Description	• Confused • Unbelieving	• Dependent • Immature	• Independent • Maturing	• Dependable • Mature
Language	Meistic	I oriented	We oriented	Others oriented

NOTES

Chapter 1: Where It All Began

1. Robert L. Thomas and Stanley N. Gundry, *A Harmony of the Gospels* (Chicago: Moody, 1978).

2. Dann Spader, *Harmony Study.* http://www.sonlife.com.

3. The four books I'm referencing here are A. B. Bruce, *The Training of the Twelve* (CreateSpace Independent Publishing Platform, 2012); Carl Wilson, *With Christ in the School of Disciple Building: The Ministry Methods of Jesus* (Andragathia Inc. Ministries, 2012); Bill Hull, *Jesus Christ, Disciple Maker* (Grand Rapids: Baker Books, 2004); and then possibly Robert Coleman, *The Master Plan of Evangelism* Second Edition, (Grand Rapids: Revell, 2010), even though this is more of an identification of some principles from Jesus's life instead of a study of His process of disciple-making.

Chapter 2: The Full Humanity of Jesus

1. Philip Schaff, *Creeds of Christendom*, CCEL, Volume 2, Symbolum Chalcedonense, 62–63.

2. Bruce Ware, quoted from a message preached at Christ Community Church in St. Charles, Illinois, on November 12, 1996.

3. Or as Augustine said, "If you diminish His humanity, then you diminish what He did for us. If you make Him less than human, our salvation is less than complete." For one of the best devotionals on this subject that treats well both the chronology and humanity of Jesus at the same time, see J. Oswald Sanders, *The Incomparable Christ* (Chicago: Moody, 1952).

4. From a message preached at Christ Community Church in St. Charles, Illinois, on November 12, 1996. See also Bruce Ware, *The Man Christ Jesus: Theological Reflections on the Humanity of Christ* (Wheaton, IL: Crossway Books, 2013).

Chapter 3: Our Mission and Motive

1. In the Greek language, these are called participial phrases.

Chapter 4: The Method—an Overview

1. Bargil Pixner, *With Jesus Through Galilee* (Israel: Corazin Publishing, 1992).

2. While many harmonies will also add in here Luke 5:1–11 as a parallel passage, it is clear from the text that this is a different event that happened later and for a different purpose. It is important to realize this is a second challenge to follow Him and not a parallel passage.

3. I'm indebted to Jim Putnam here for his friendship, preaching, and excellent workbook. Jim Putnam, *Real-Life Discipleship: Building Churches that Make Disciples* (Wheaton, IL: NavPress, 2010).

4. See Dann Spader, *Knowing Him.* http://www.sonlife.com. See days 15–20 in the study.

5. The hymn they sang is from the Hillel Psalms. Psalm 118 was always sung at the end of the meal. The psalm says, "The stone the builders rejected has become the capstone." Imagine how Jesus would have felt as He sang this song right before He goes to the Cross.

Chapter 5: Chair 1: The Lost

1. Taken from a recorded message played in part on "The Land and the Book" radio program by Charlie Dyer on April 20, 2013.

2. Traditionally, we call Jesus a "carpenter" because this is how the Bible has translated the Greek word *tekton* for years. *Tekton* is probably better translated as "master craftsman." This probably involved stone-cutting and maybe some carpentry, as all the building in the days of Jesus were stone buildings.

3. Dann Spader, *Knowing God Personally.* http://sonlife.com.

Chapter 6: Chair 2: The Believer

1. Sonlife Ministries conducts training seminars for youth pastors, pastors, and church leaders called the "Muvement Seminar, a strategy for building a movement of disciple makers." It is an overview of Christ's life and how He created a movement of multiplying disciples. It looks at the timeline of Christ's life and what He did the first year, the second year, and the third and fourth year. See http://www.sonlife.com.

2. See http://www.WalkingasJesus.com for a ten-week study, free videos, and downloads.

3. Ann Spangler and Lois Tverberg, *Sitting at the Feet of Rabbi Jesus: How the Jewishness of Jesus Can Transform Your Faith* (Grand Rapids: Zondervan, 2009).

4. Dann Spader, *33 Things that Happen at the Moment of Salvation.* http://www.sonlife.com.

Chapter 7: Chair 3: The Worker

1. Billy Graham Institute of Evangelism, *Disciple Making: A Self Study Course* (Wheaton, IL: Billy Graham Center, 1994).

2. Many harmonies want to pull Luke 5:1–11 out of the normal order Luke gives it and place it parallel to Mark 1:6–20 and Matthew 4:18–22. But it is obviously a different event at a different time and conveys several new insights about working with disciples at this stage of the journey.

3. Some would also argue that the John 5 "feast of the Jews" could have happened just prior to His rejection at Nazareth. While it is impossible to clearly date this event or which feast it is, this would change the flow of events. If the rejection in Jerusalem by the religious leaders was just prior to His rejection in His hometown, these factors would frame up Jesus's decision to make a strategic decision to "move with the movers" and invest in those who were most eager to learn.

4. Apollos was a native of Alexandria and traveled to Ephesus. He spoke with "great fervor . . . though he knew only the baptism of John" (Acts 18:24–25).

5. Bargil Pixner, *With Jesus Through Galilee* (Israel: Corazin Publishing, 1992).

Chapter 8: Chair 4: The Disciple-Maker

1. Carl Wilson, *With Christ in the School of Disciple Building: The Ministry Methods of Jesus* (Andragathia Inc. Ministries, 2012).

2. Dann Spader, *The Cost of Leading Movements of Multiplication*. http://www.sonlife.com.

Chapter 9: Sticking Points (Mark 4)

1. There are different ways to interpret this passage. Please don't let a different viewpoint cause you to miss the observations suggested here. Many hold that only the last person (the good soil) is a true believer, because only the last soil produces fruit. But if you look at this parable from the lens of first-century farmers, plus combine it with John 12:24 where the germination of the seed is the beginning of growth toward fruit-bearing, other interpretations become possible. Even though the plant growing on the rocky soil or thorny soil may not produce fruit, the seed has germinated and is growing toward eventually fruit-bearing, but it is stopped before fruit arrives. The seed sown on the rocky soil and the thorny soil does germinate and is alive, it just never produces fruit due to other circumstances in life.

Chapter 10: Barriers between Chairs (John 15)

1. Juan Carlos Ortiz, *Call to Discipleship* (Logos International, 1975).

Appendix 1: For Elders and Overseers

1. Acts 11:30; 14:23; 15:2–6, 22–23; 16:4; 20:17–38; 21:17–26; Ephesians 4:11; Philippians 1:1; 1 Timothy 3:1–7; 4:14; 5:17–25; Titus 1:5–9; James 5:13–15; 1 Peter 5:1–5. (See also John 10:1–10; 21:15–17; 1 Thessalonians 5:12–13; Hebrews 13:17.) For an exegesis of most of these passages I suggest Alexander Strauch, *Biblical Eldership: An Urgent Call to Restore Biblical Church Leadership* (Colorado Springs: Lewis and Roth Publishers, 1995).

Appendix 2: Building a Disciple-Making Ministry

1. Sonlife's 7-hour "Muvement" training (strategy seminar) is an overview of how Christ, as a leader, built a movement of multiplying disciples. Sonlife also has developed its "Live 2:6" training that is up to an additional twelve days of training on how to build a movement of disciple-makers as seen in the life of Christ. http://www.sonlife.com.

2. Dann Spader, *Walking as Jesus Walked: Making Disciples the Way Jesus Did* (Chicago: Moody Publishers, 2011).

Sonlife

Muvement
Seminars

A Strategy for **Making** and **Multiplying** Disciples as Jesus did...

Sonlife Ministries conducts leadership seminars called

Muvement:
A Strategy for Making and Multiplying Disciples as Jesus did.

These events can be brought to your church or area and are normally 6-8 hours in length. They cover the 4 Chairs, plus give an overview of how Jesus built a movement of multiplying disciples.

THE SEMINAR INCLUDES TOPICS SUCH AS:
— What is our mission?
— What is our motive?
— Why is Jesus our model?
— What does a disciple look like?
— How did Jesus create a movement of multiplying disciples?

Host or find a seminar near you by visiting our website: Sonlife.com
Each Muvement attendee receives a 75 page training manual and a Sonlife certified trainer.

Sonlife.com

ISBN 978-0-8024-4709-8

Want to start making disciples in your church?

Encourage the people around you to know the life of Christ. Start that knowledge by taking a small group through *Walking as Jesus Walked*, also by Dann Spader.

Learn to obey as Jesus obeyed, pray as Jesus prayed, and have intentional, loving relationships as Jesus did with those around Him.

also available as an ebook

MOODY
Publishers™

From the Word to Life

THE NAME YOU CAN TRUST®

MOODYRADIO

Where you turn. For life.

Moody Radio produces and delivers compelling programs filled with biblical insights and creative expressions of faith that help you take the next step in your relationship with Christ.

You can hear Moody Radio on 36 stations and more than 1,500 radio outlets across the U.S. and Canada. Or listen on your smartphone with the Moody Radio app!

www.moodyradio.org